Hi everyone,

Once again, thank you for purchasing our coloring book. We hope that you enjoy this book. For more inquiries or concerns, please don't hesitate to contact us at kreatif@blondea.com

We highly recommended taking a screenshot or photography by sharing your coloring pages on the internet. We will be happy to see your posts. Feel free to share your art and tag us on any social media #kreatifworldcoloring

Our professional team published numerous coloring books. So, ensure that you explore the whole collection and find a great book you desire for your next color.

Leave Your Amazon Review

Please share your experience and help other colorists to discover our coloring book. Find this book on Amazon, scroll to the customer reviews to share your opinions.

We appreciate your purchase and reviews. It will help us to keep improving as well.

Cheers,
Kreatifworld Coloring Team

©2020 KreatifWorld. All rights reserved
Contact: kreatif@blondea.com

THE POWER OF MANDALA

The word mandala originated from the Hindu religion used for Buddhist practice. The term Mandala comes from a Sanskrit word, which means circle. During ancient times, it was used for medicine by the Native American and Eastern world. It used for healing body, spirit, and soul. The meditative aspect of Mandala helps to bring peace to the soul. It activated by the hidden mystery of the inner mind to enrich unconditional love.

The Mandala designs can be of use for many purposes, such as meditation, stress relief, relaxation, trance induction and creative expression.

The circle shape of Mandala fills with different symbols and geometric shapes, which displayed in symmetrical patterns with color schemes. The power of mandalas denoted with a circular design which includes:

* Represent a symbol of unity, connection, and harmony
* Calming and flowing in design
* Help to focus on the inward mind
* The center of the circle offers endless opportunities
* Reflective of circular life.

Circles represent different meanings, such as nature, wisdom, etc. Also, circles support unlimited potential that you can acquire to maintain harmony and connection. Mandalas facilitate the healing process, balancing energy, and enhancing tranquillity in the body.

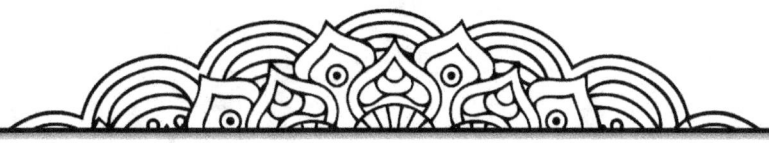

HOW TO USE THIS BOOK

Most of the coloring books include mandalas feature in relaxing nature. Also, they are easy to color, and the symmetry of the design makes it easier to achieve a good result. In other to ensure that your mandalas are stress-free to color, you can follow this useful guide below:

1. SELECT YOUR COLORS
Before start coloring, you should start by choosing the color scheme. It's a great option to start as it can be tempting to grab as many colors as possible. Limiting your color choice can genuinely make the Mandala looks more exceptional.

2. START DESIGNING FROM THE CENTER
Usually, the best Mandalas are well fitted and balanced. If you want to maintain this, it is essential to start coloring from the center and work outwards. It enables you to apply color reasonably and create a symmetrical piece.

3. USE SIMILAR COLORS FOR ANY REPEATING ELEMENTS
Ensure that you are consistent with color usage for repeating patterns in your Mandala. It creates symmetrical and balanced fittings. Any benefits of coloring from the center is that it helps to survey the whole piece quickly to identify repeating parts.

4. ADDITION OF BLENDS AND TONAL GRADIENTS
As stated earlier, it is important to limit your color choice two or four colors. Adding blends and tonal gradients help to smooth color gradations, which makes your Mandala appear more attractive and outstanding.

5. MAINTAIN RELAXATION
Take your time, enjoying the coloring process and relaxed. Let your mind focus, and allow your natural creativity flow and have fun with it. Stay positive, ease, unwind and let your worries fade away.

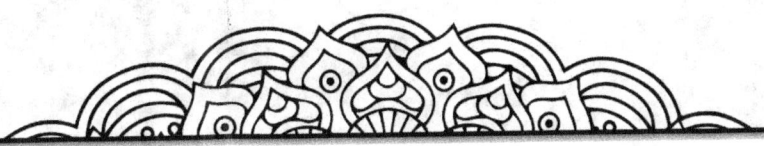

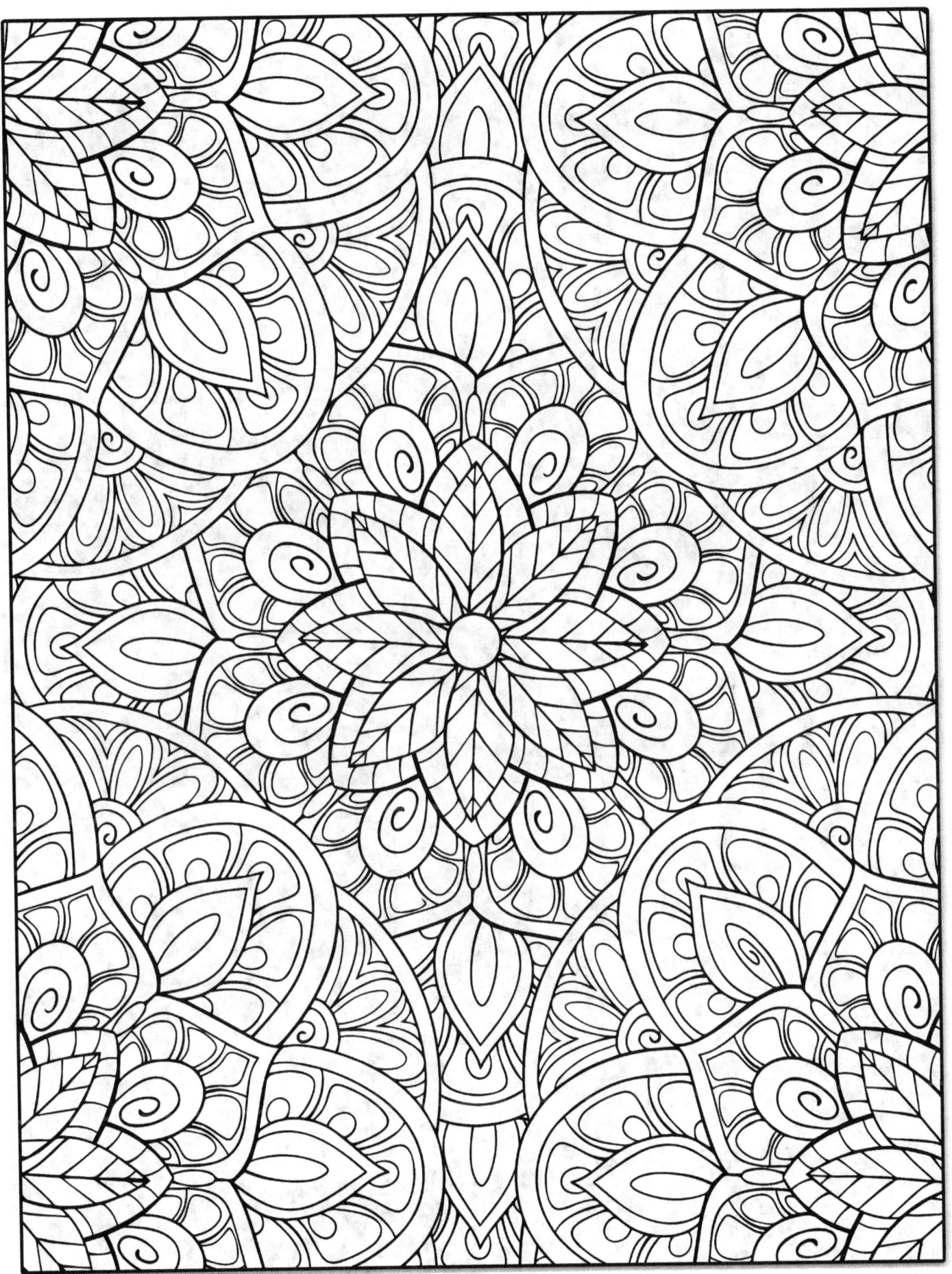

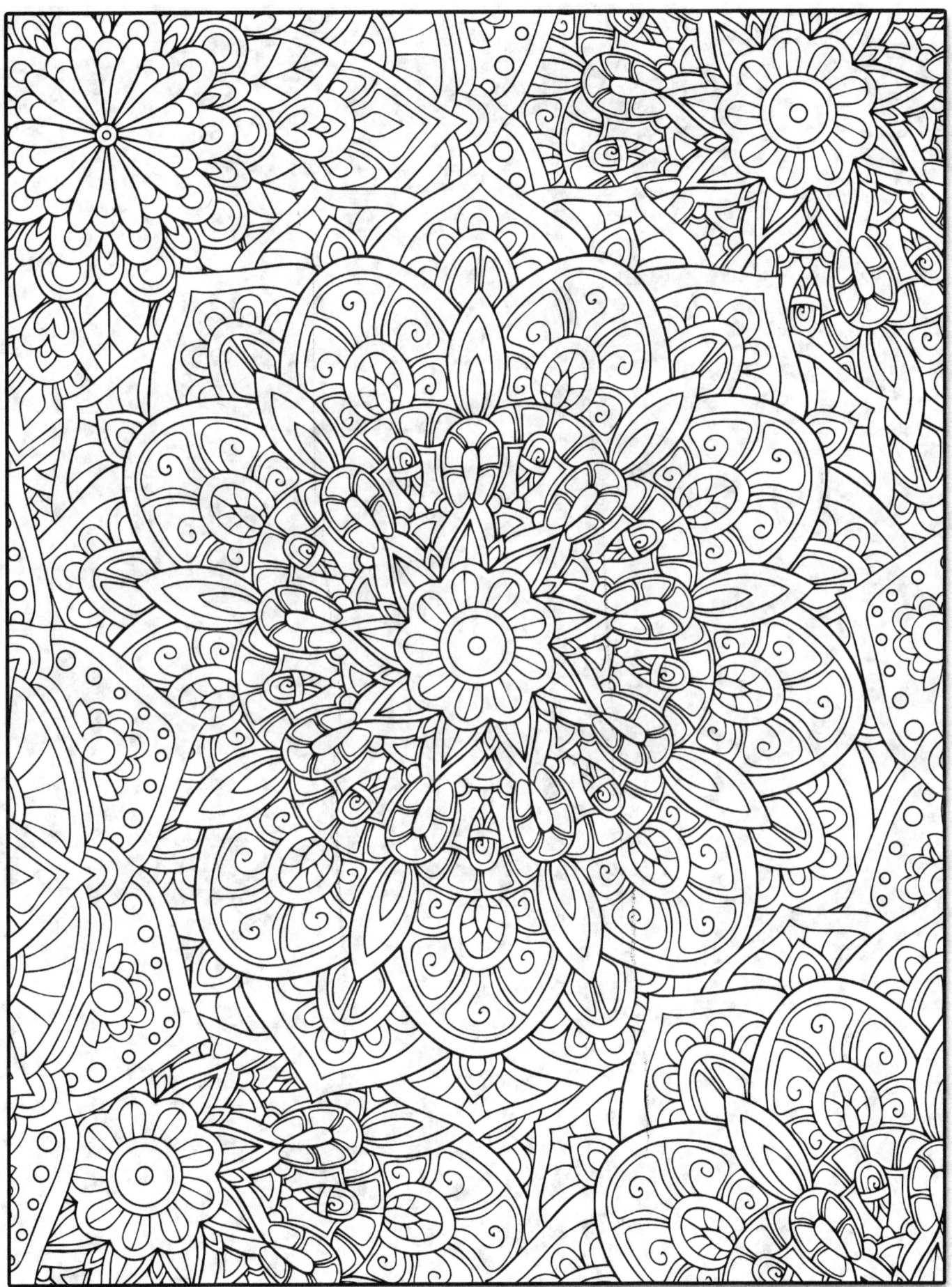

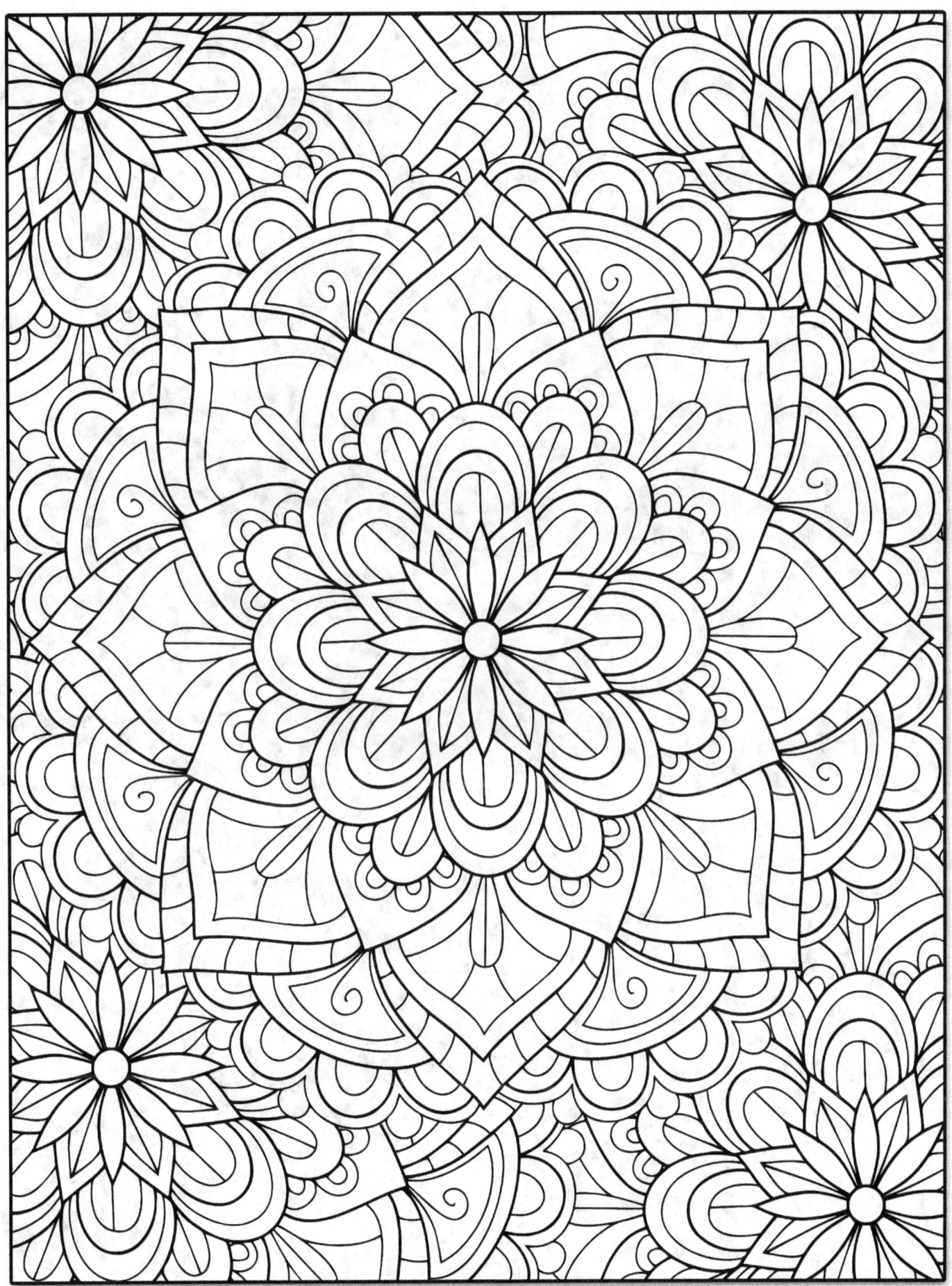

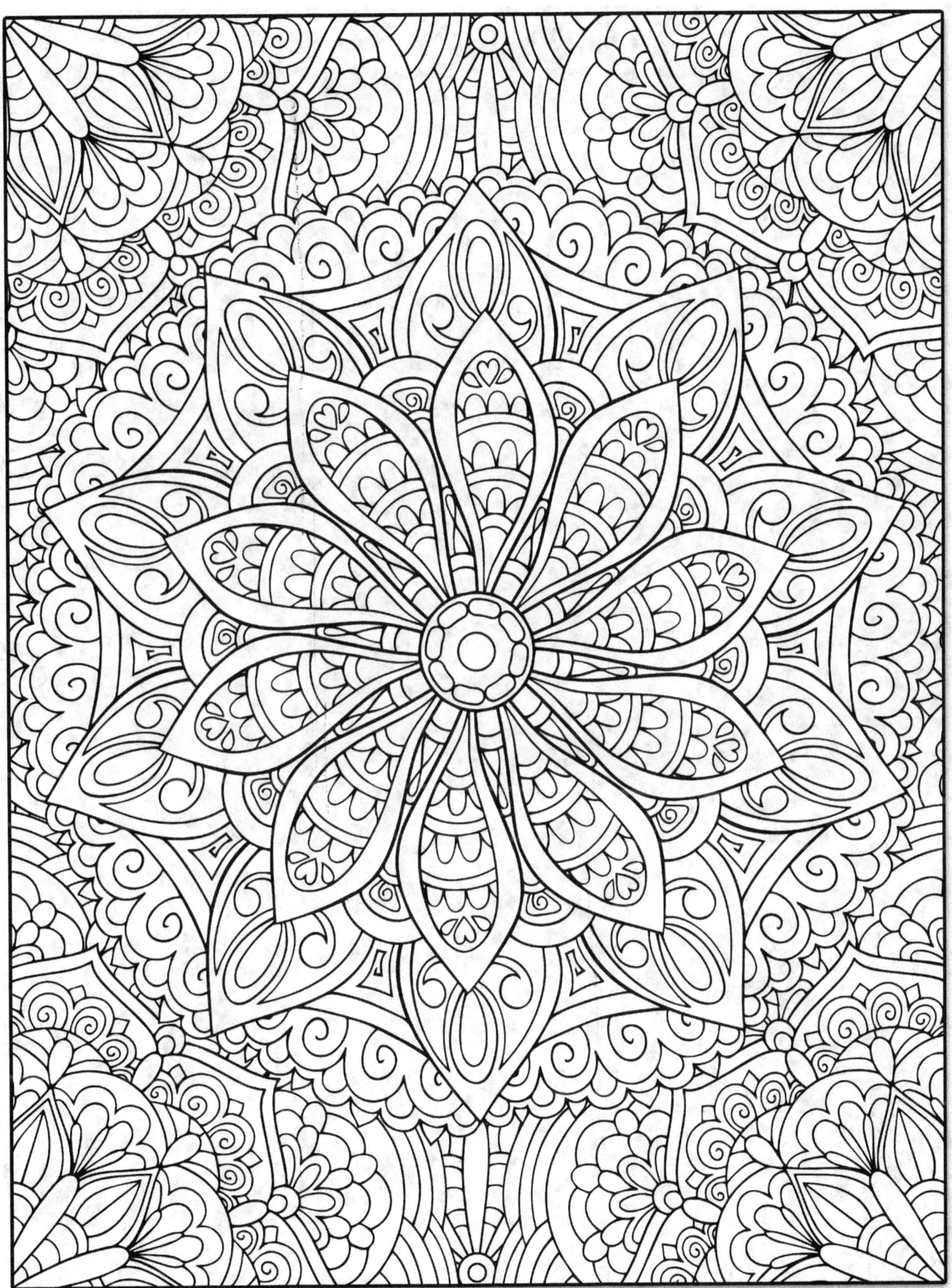

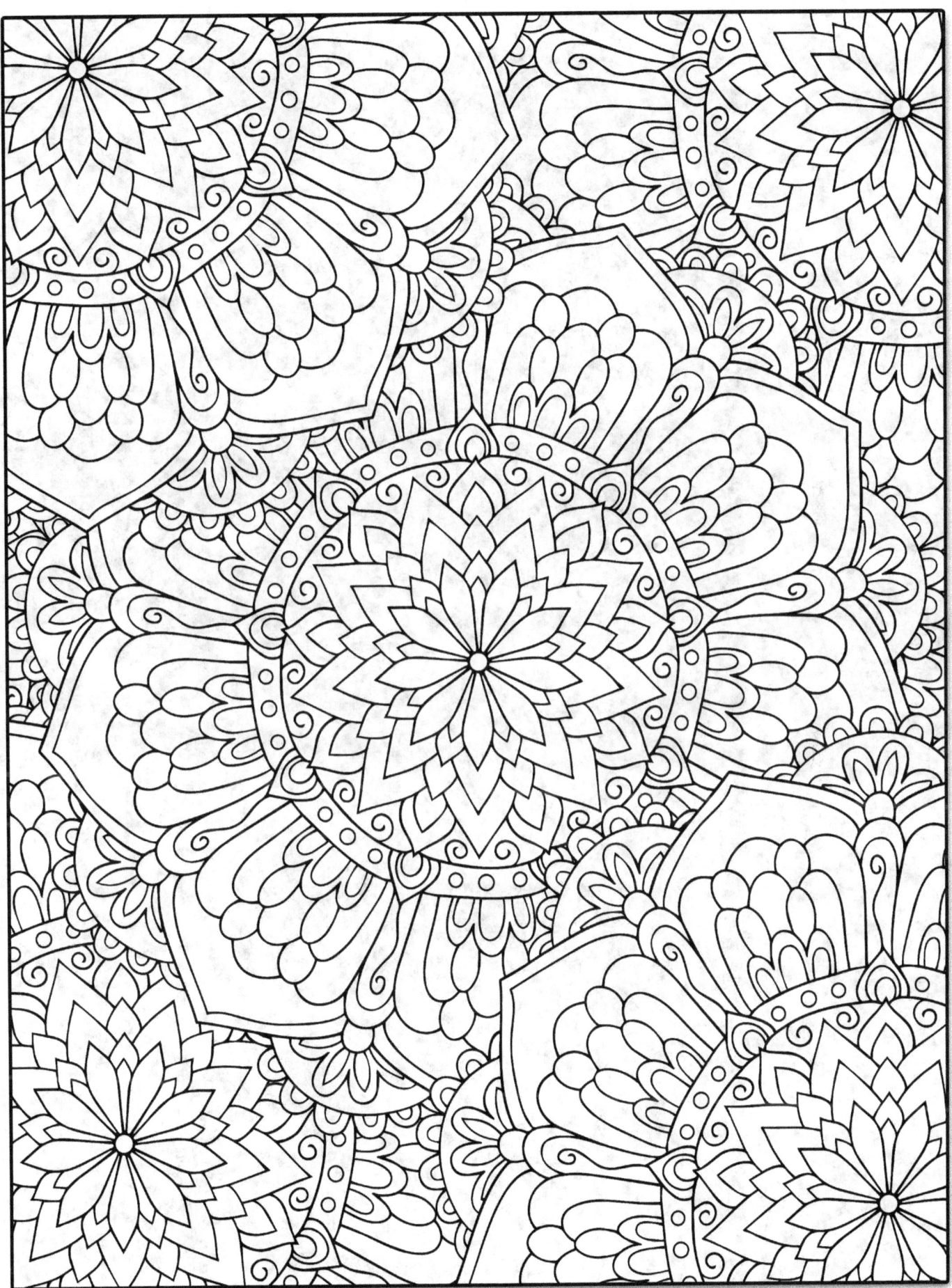

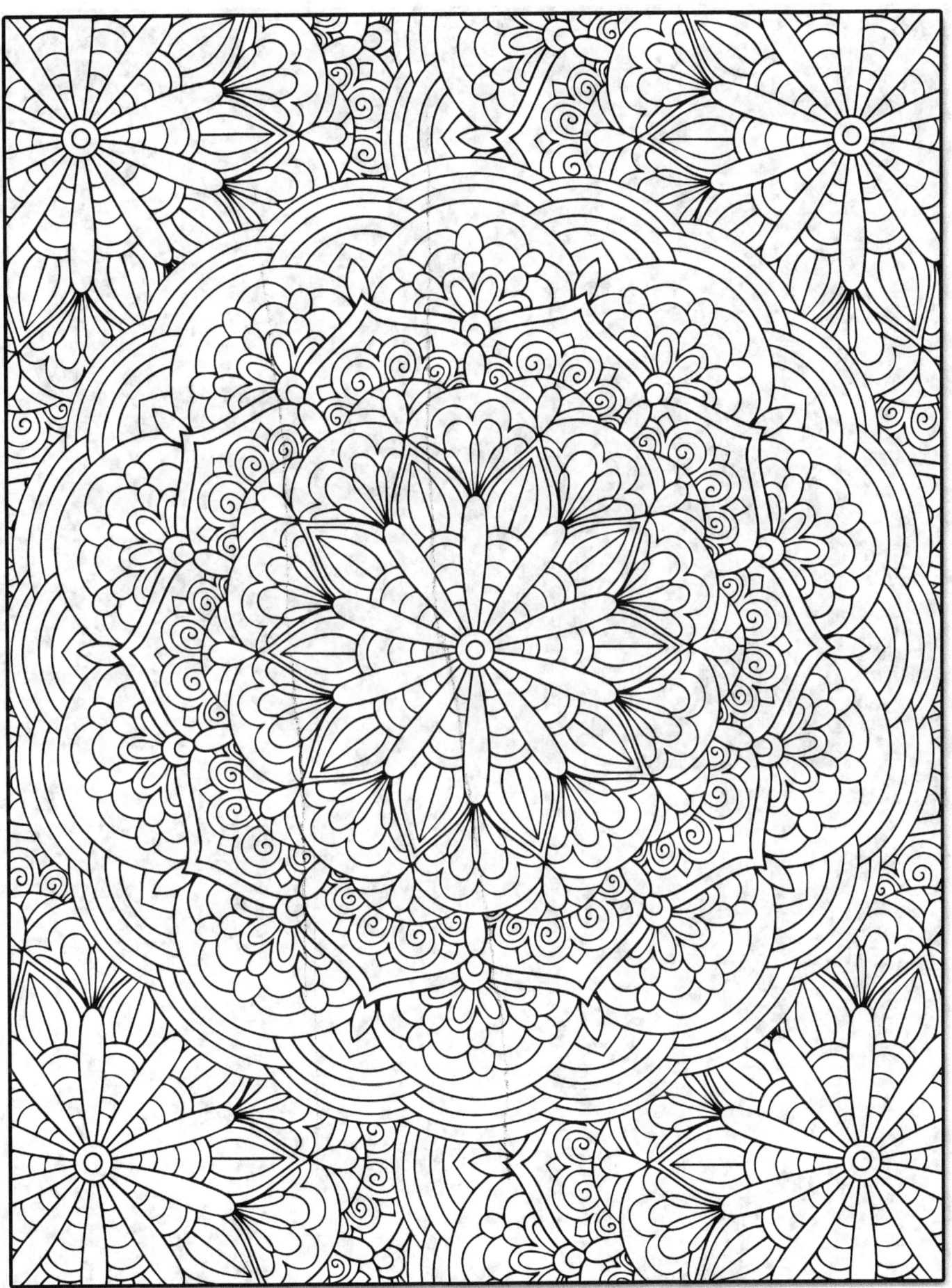

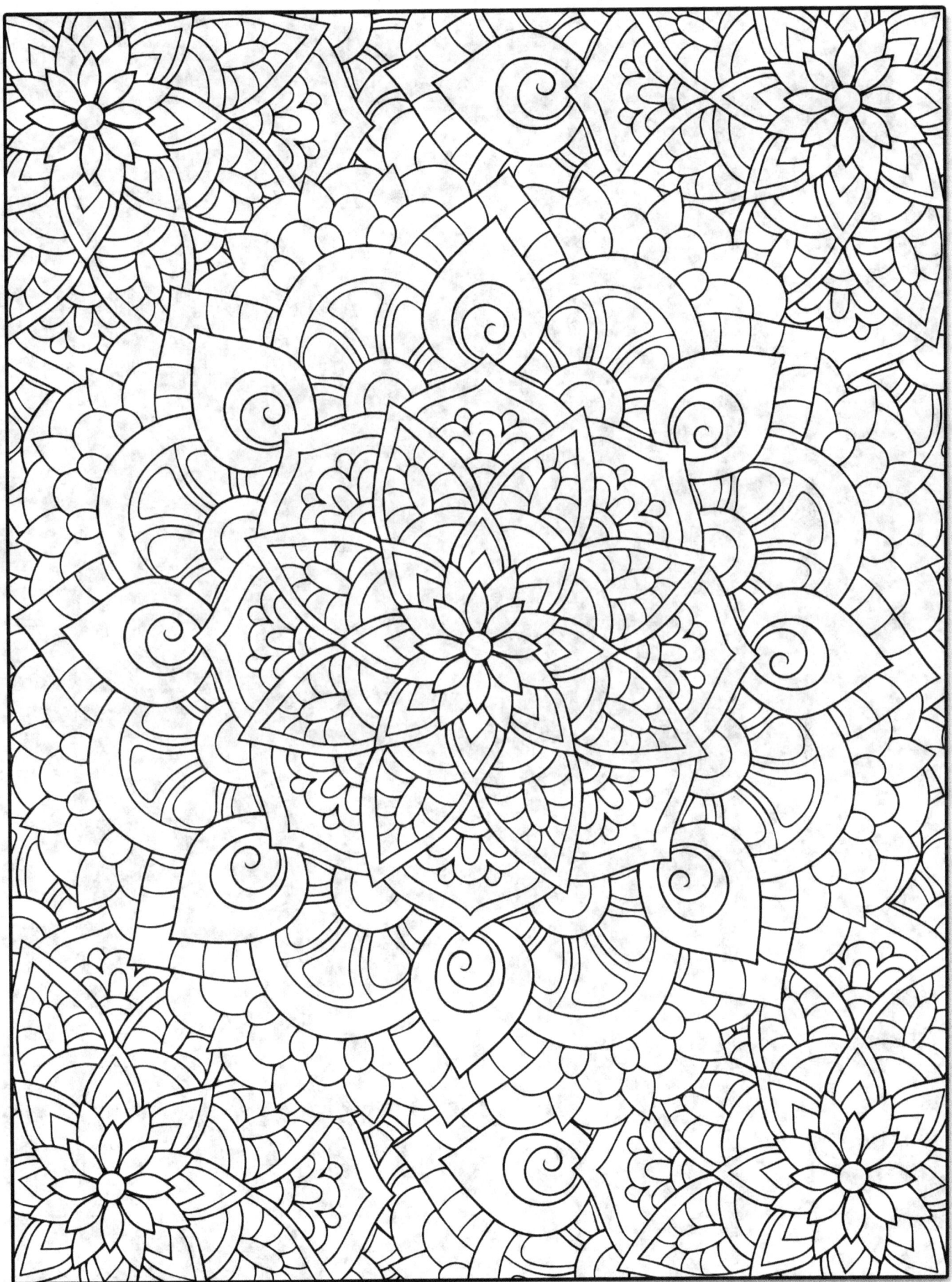

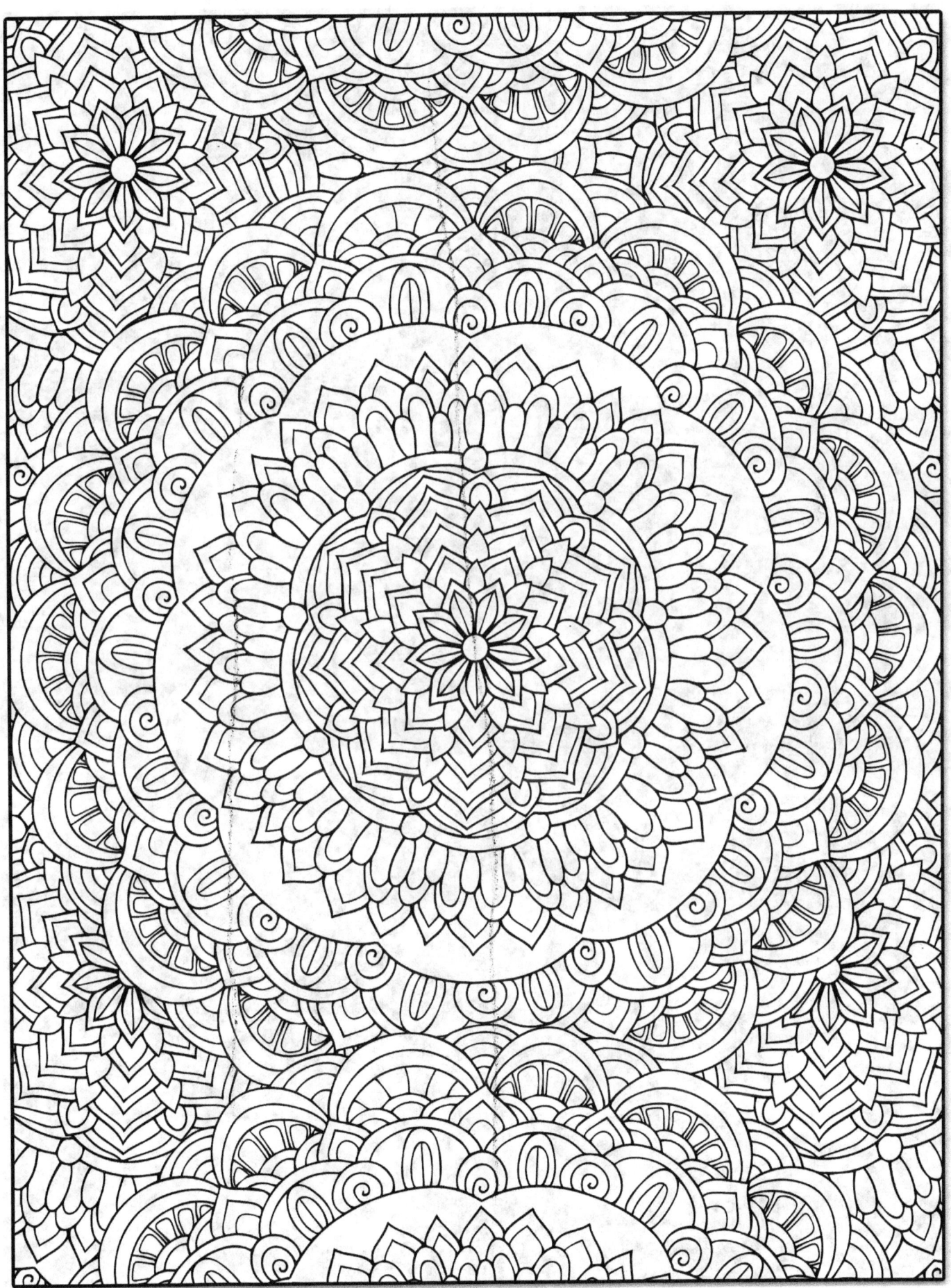

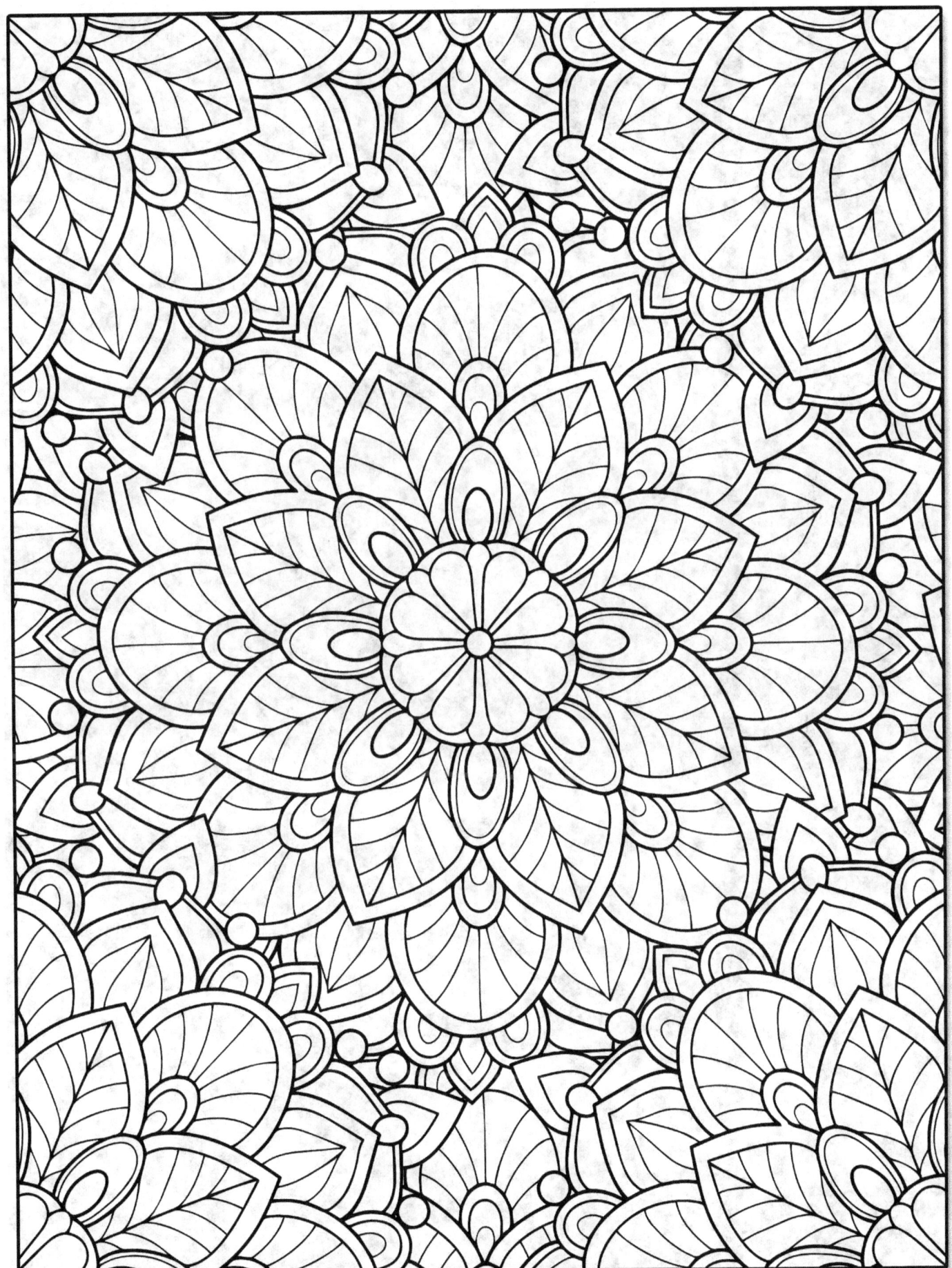

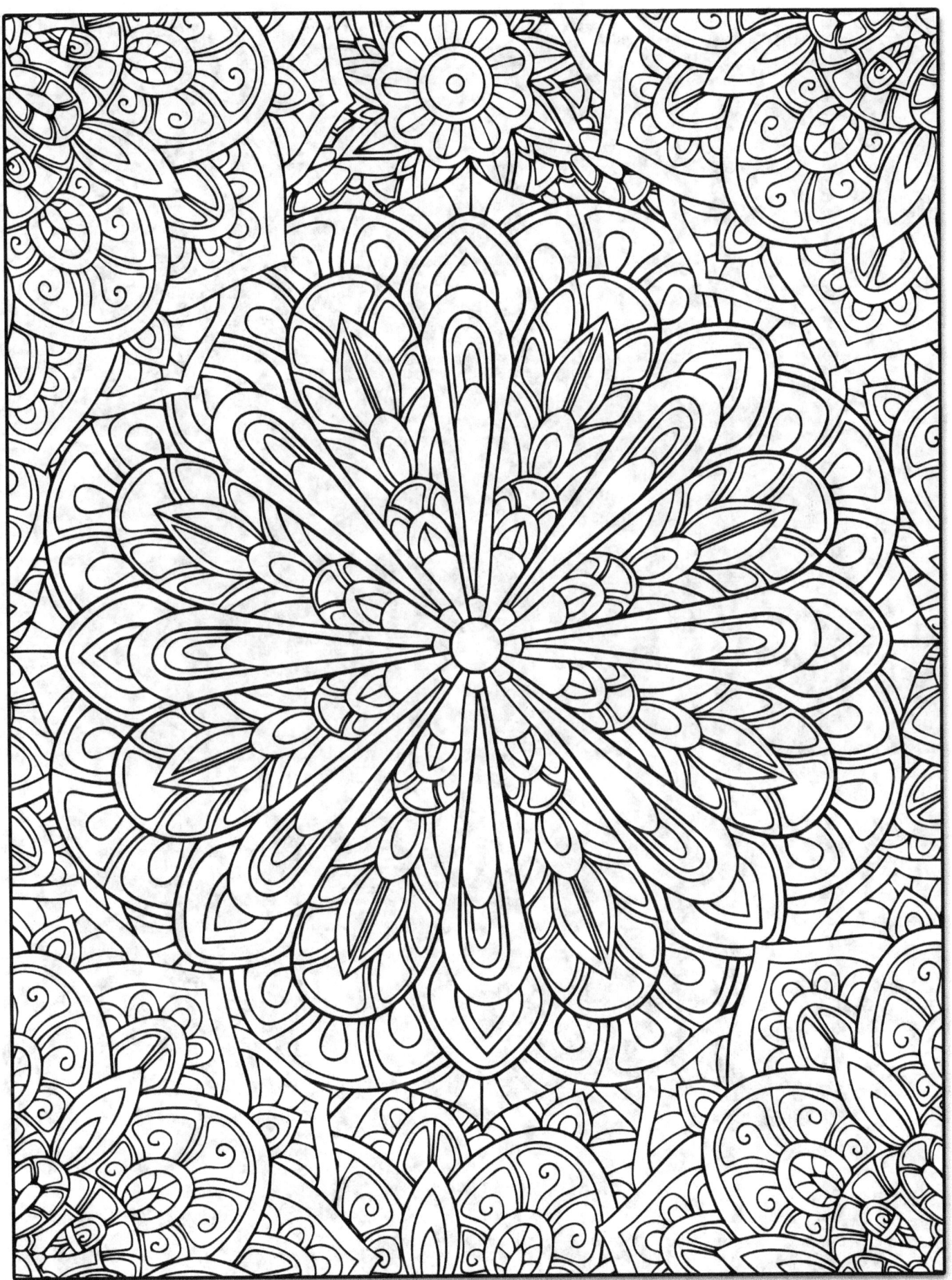

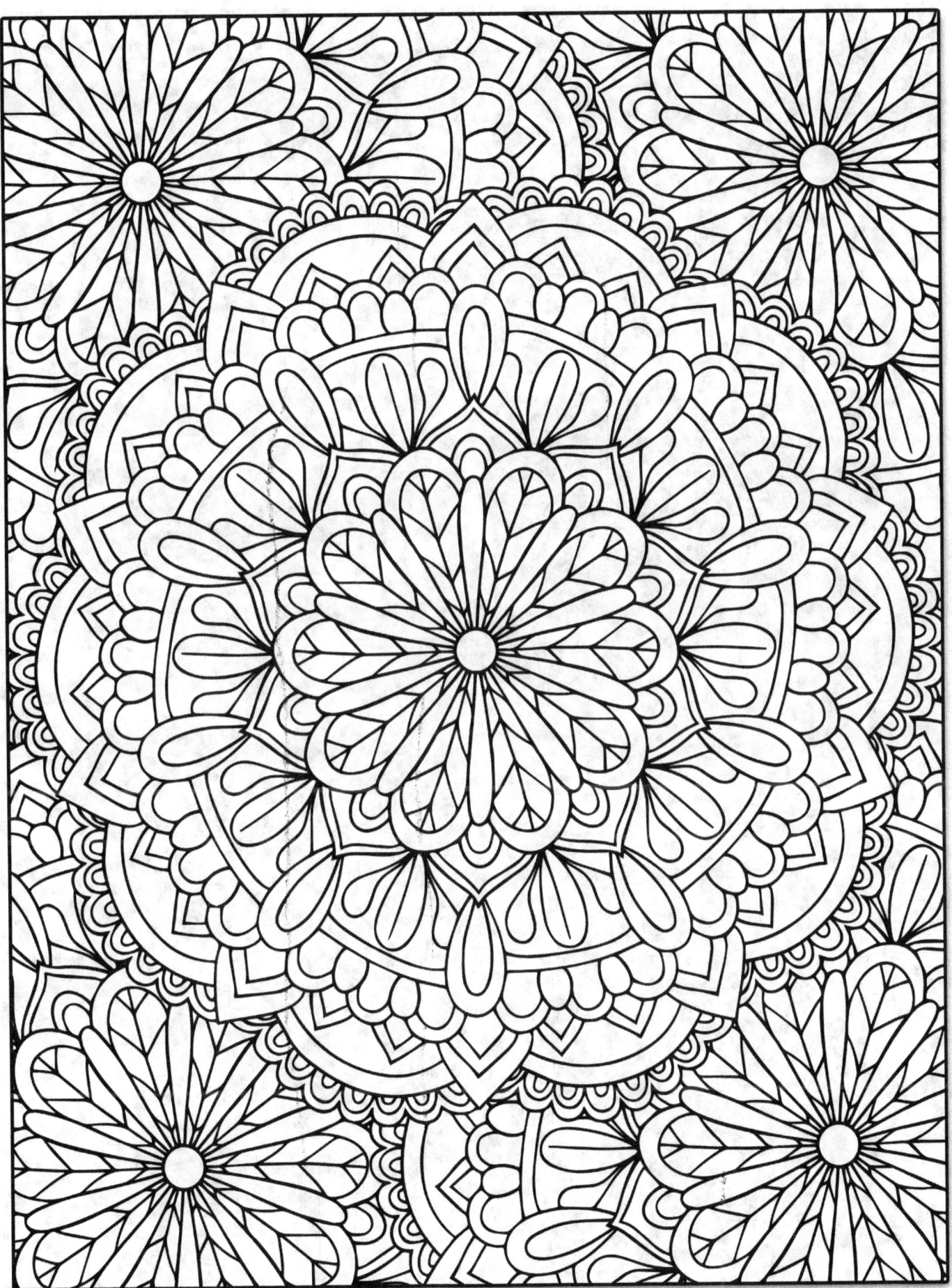

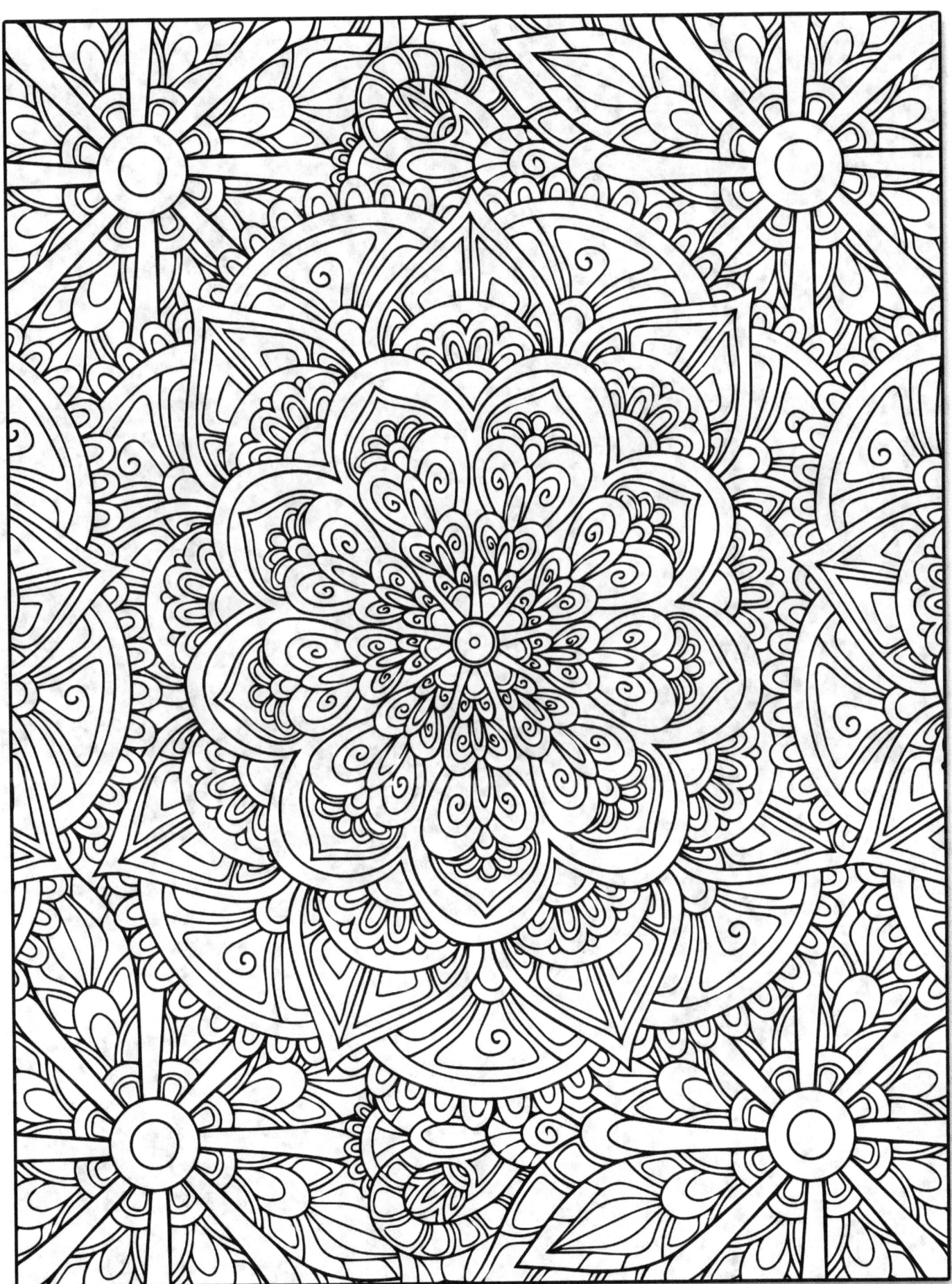

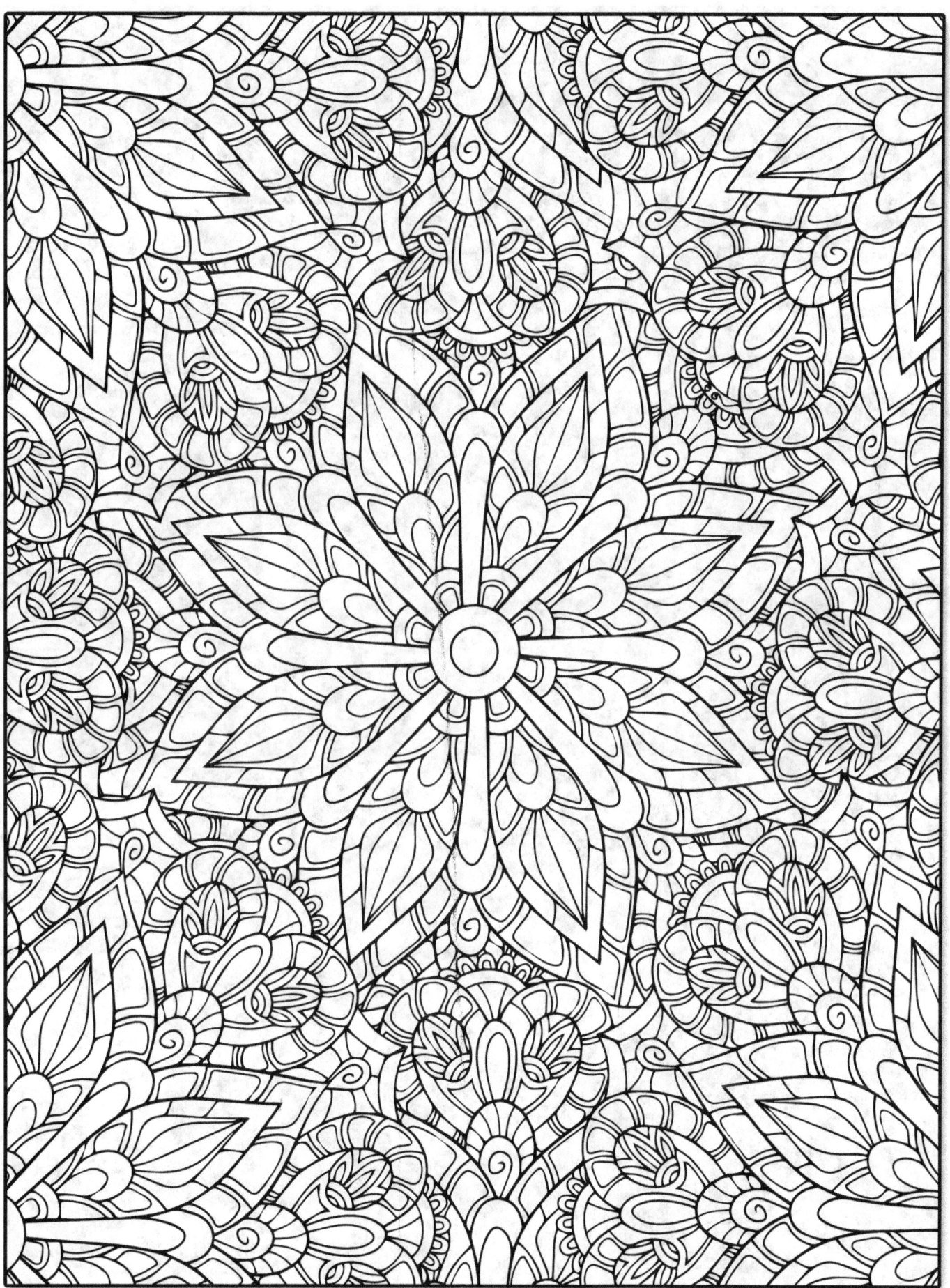

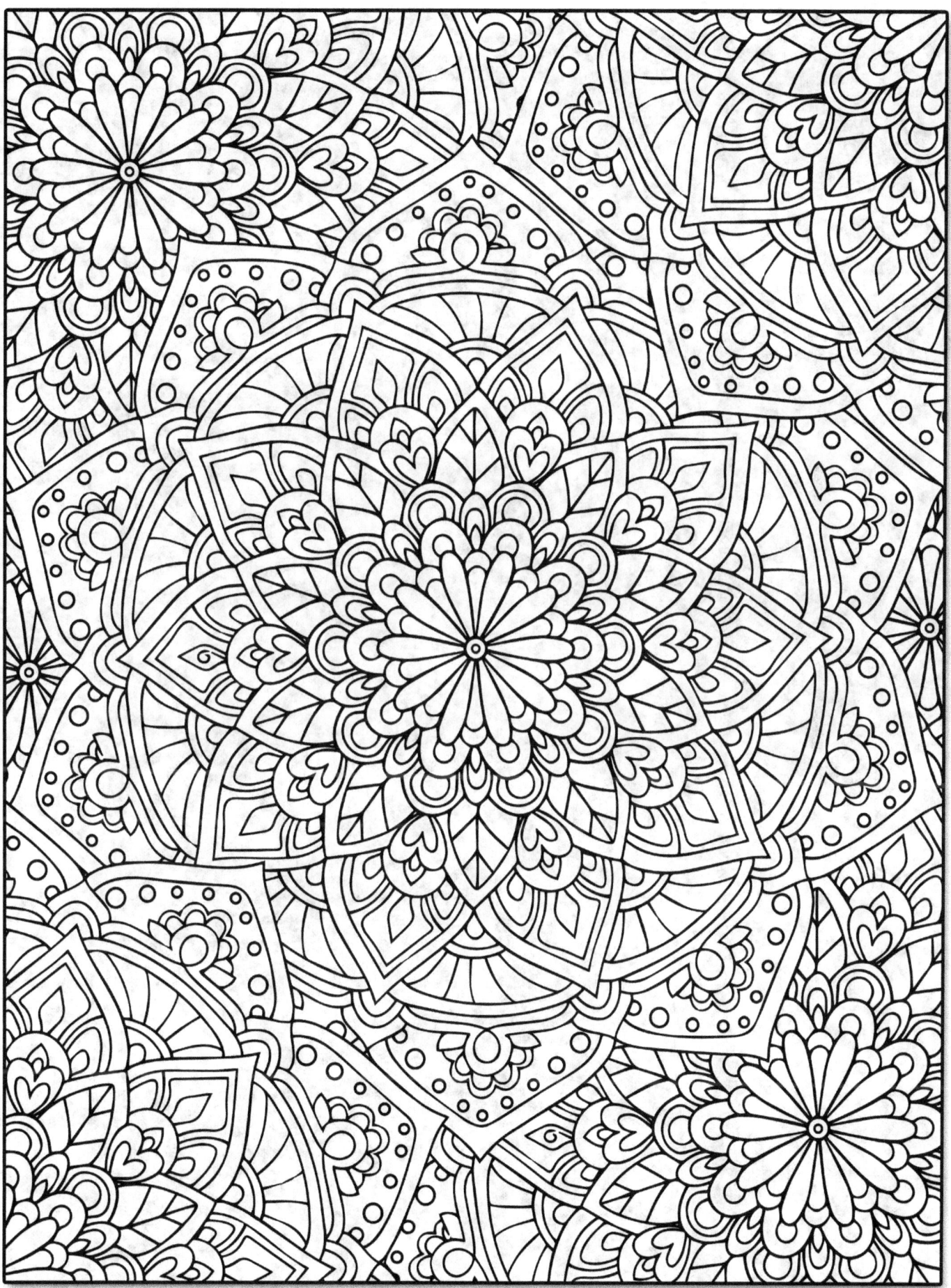

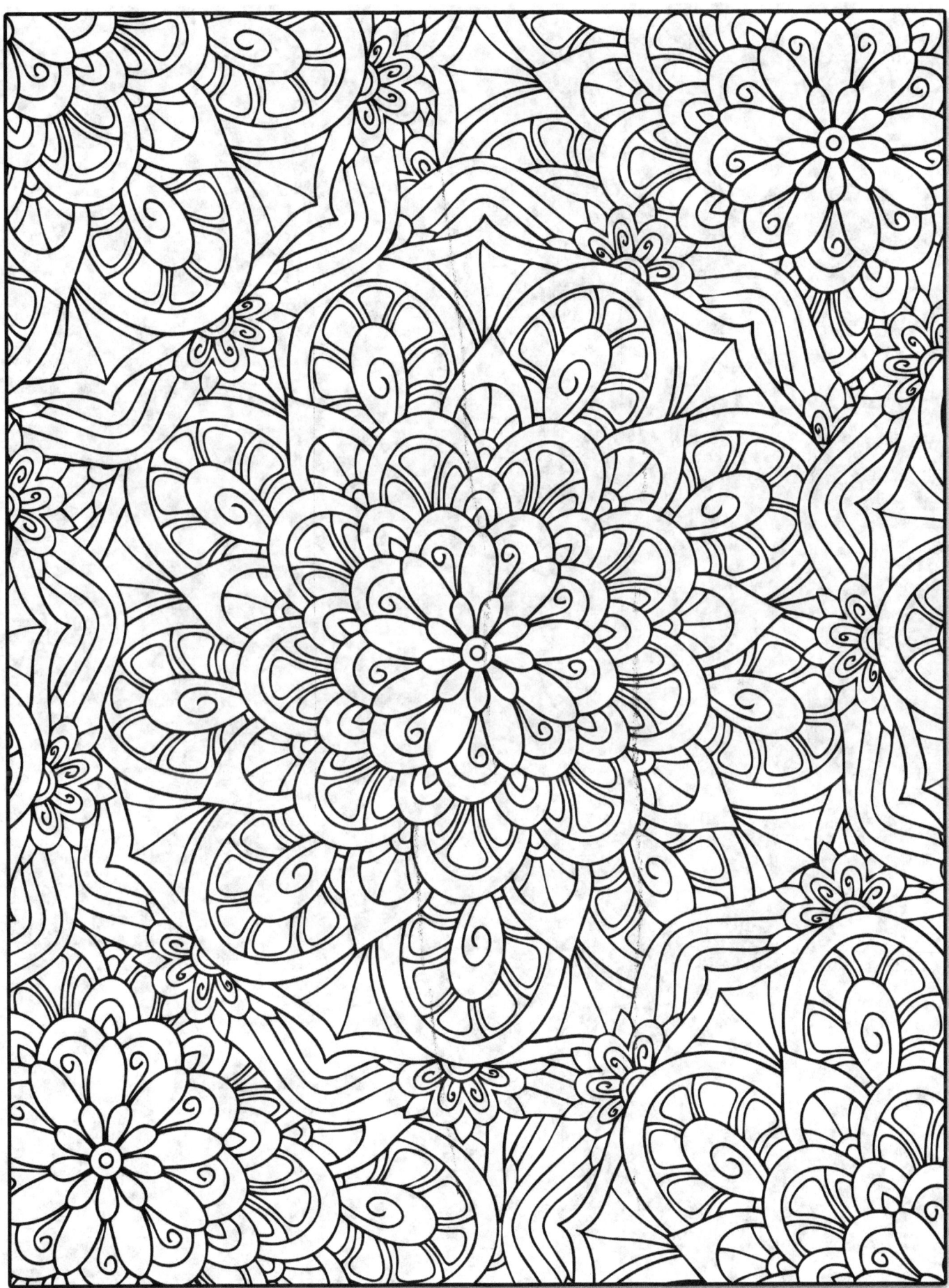

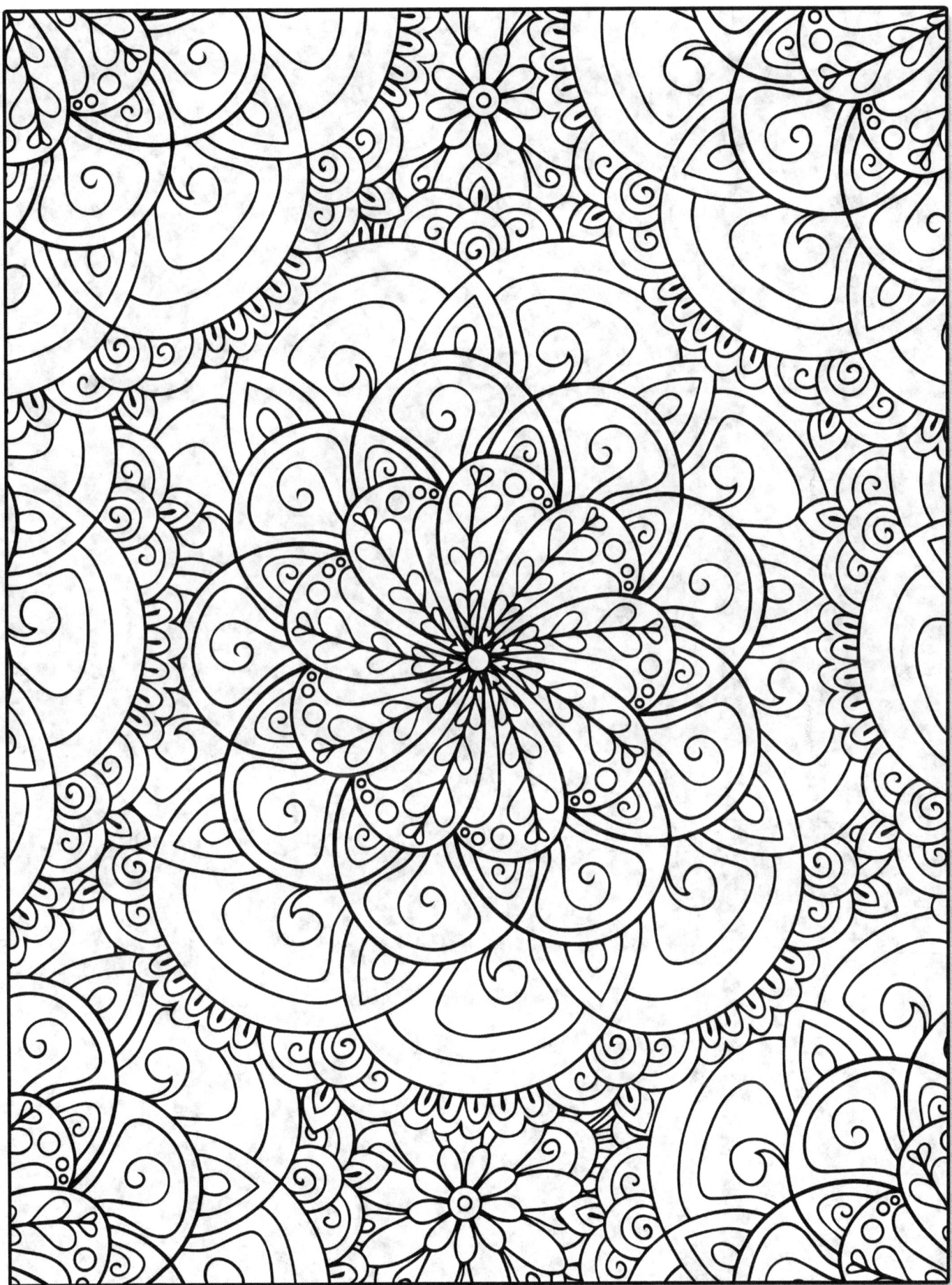

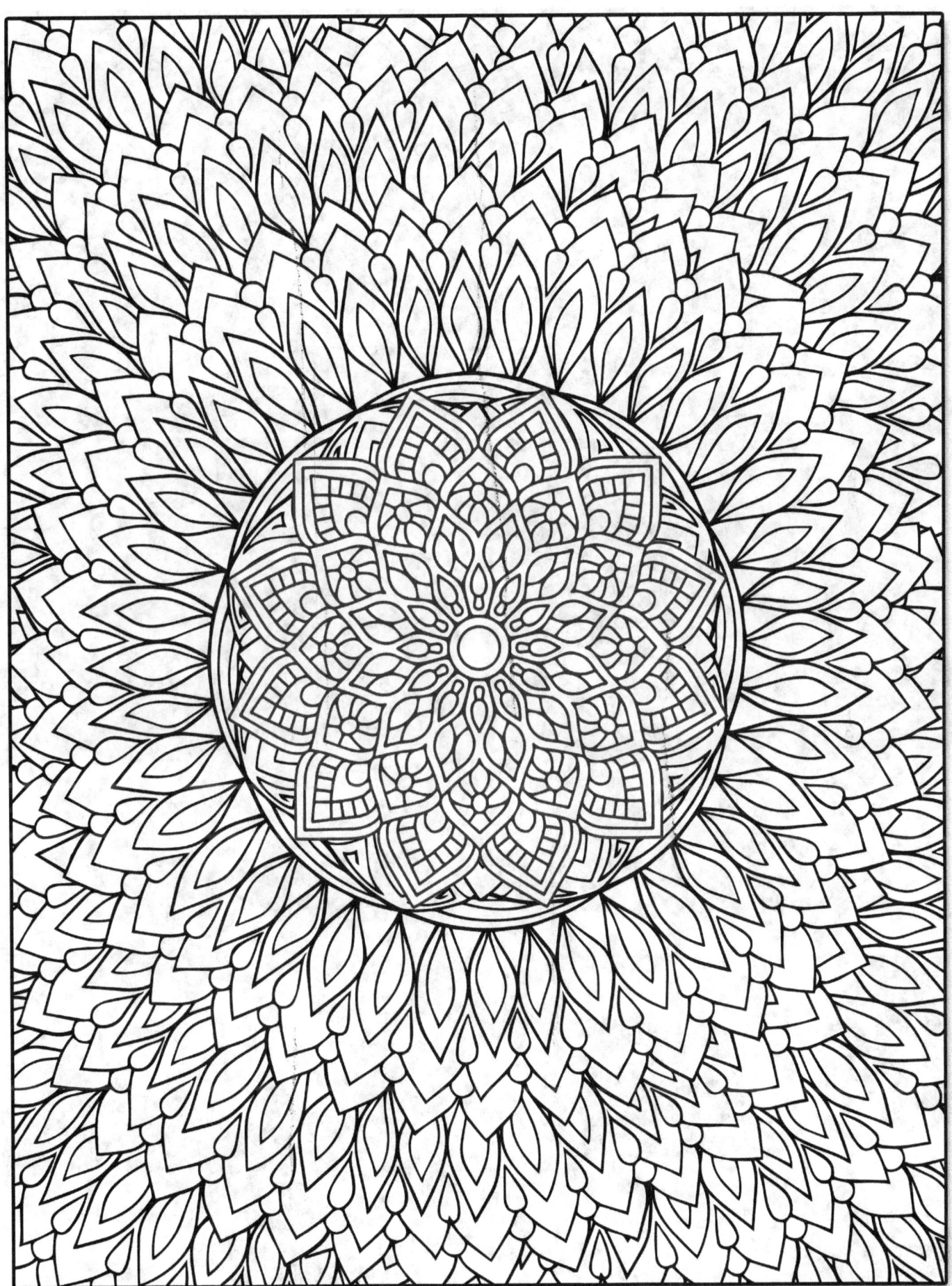

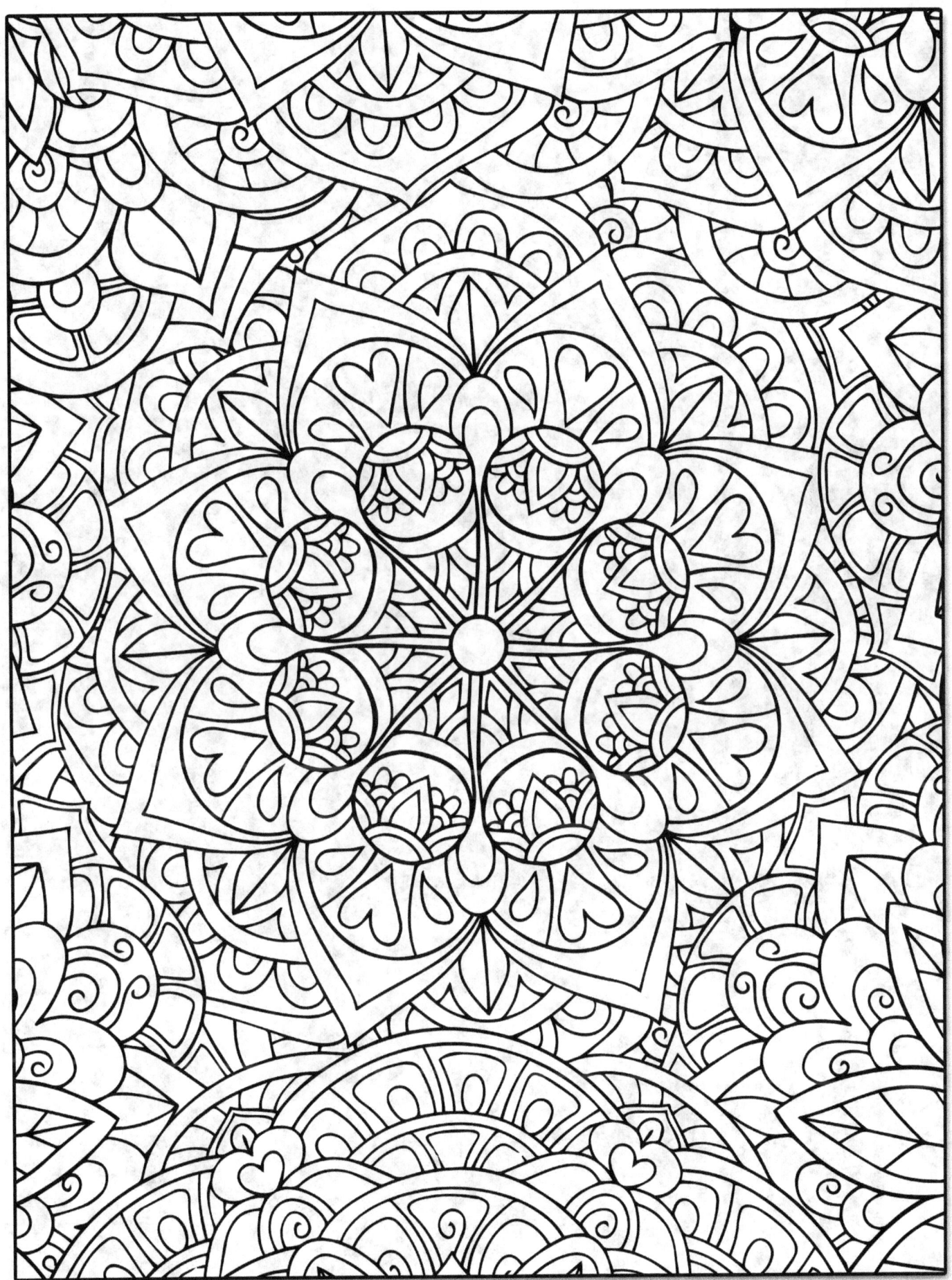

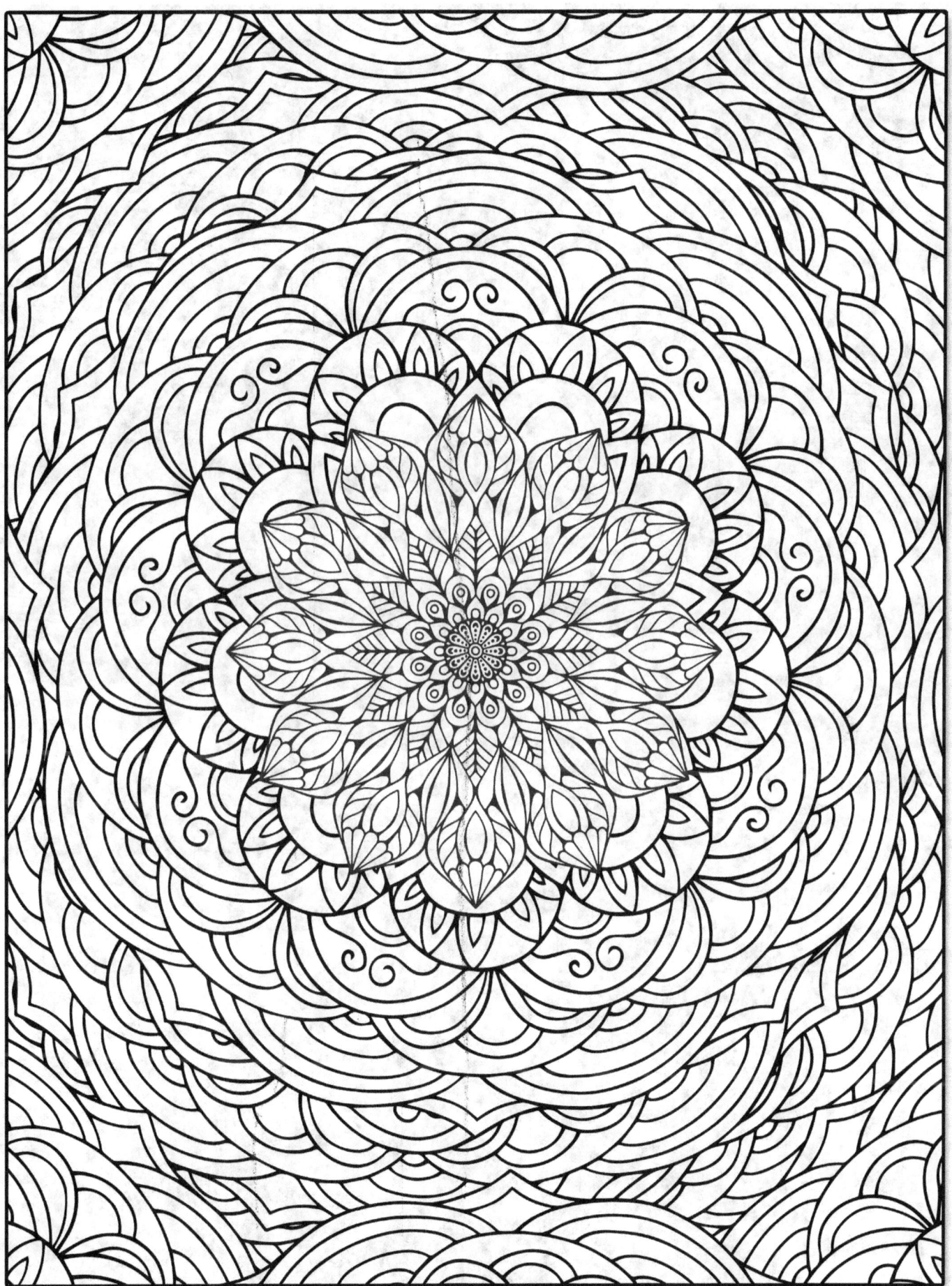

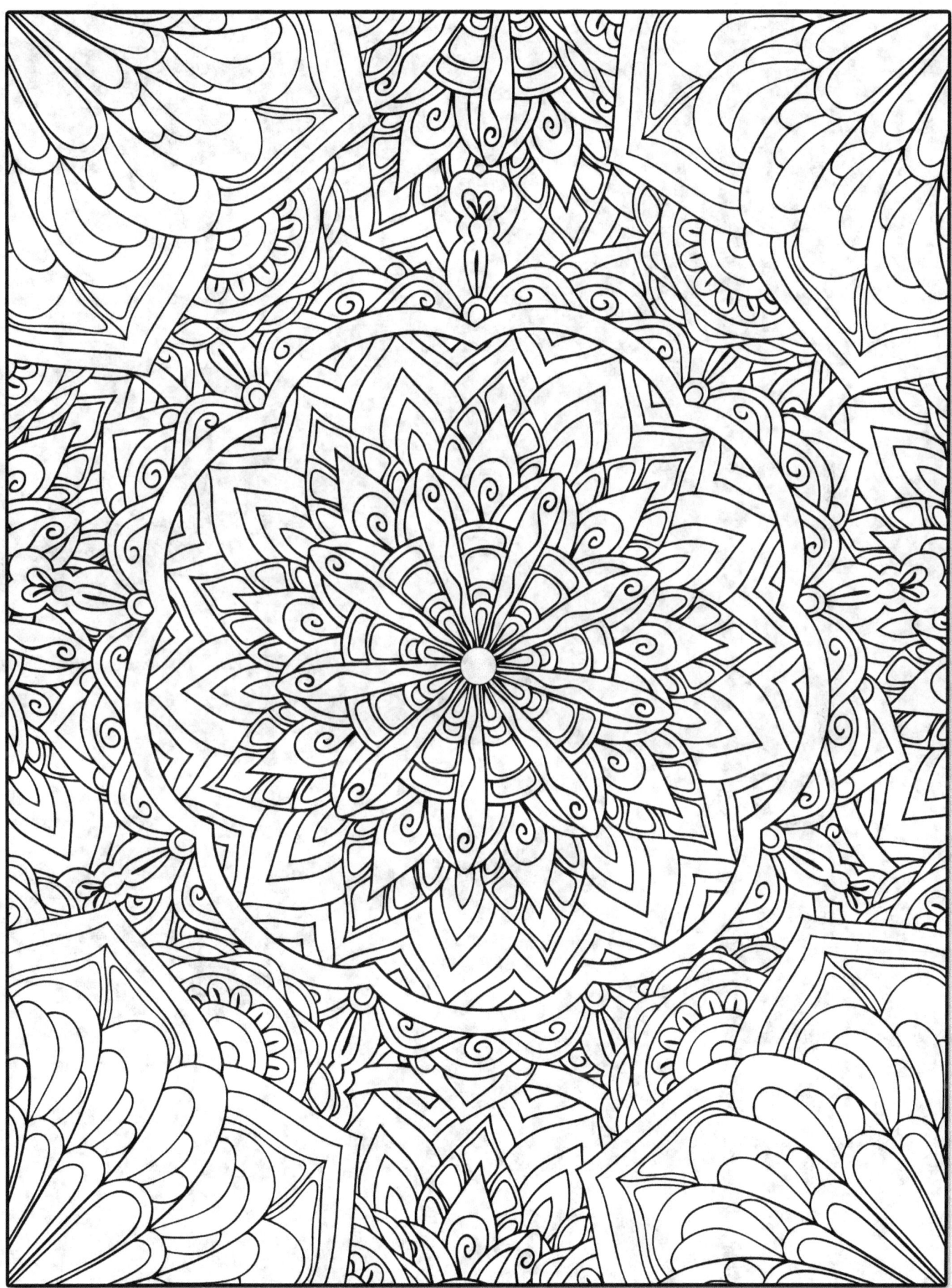

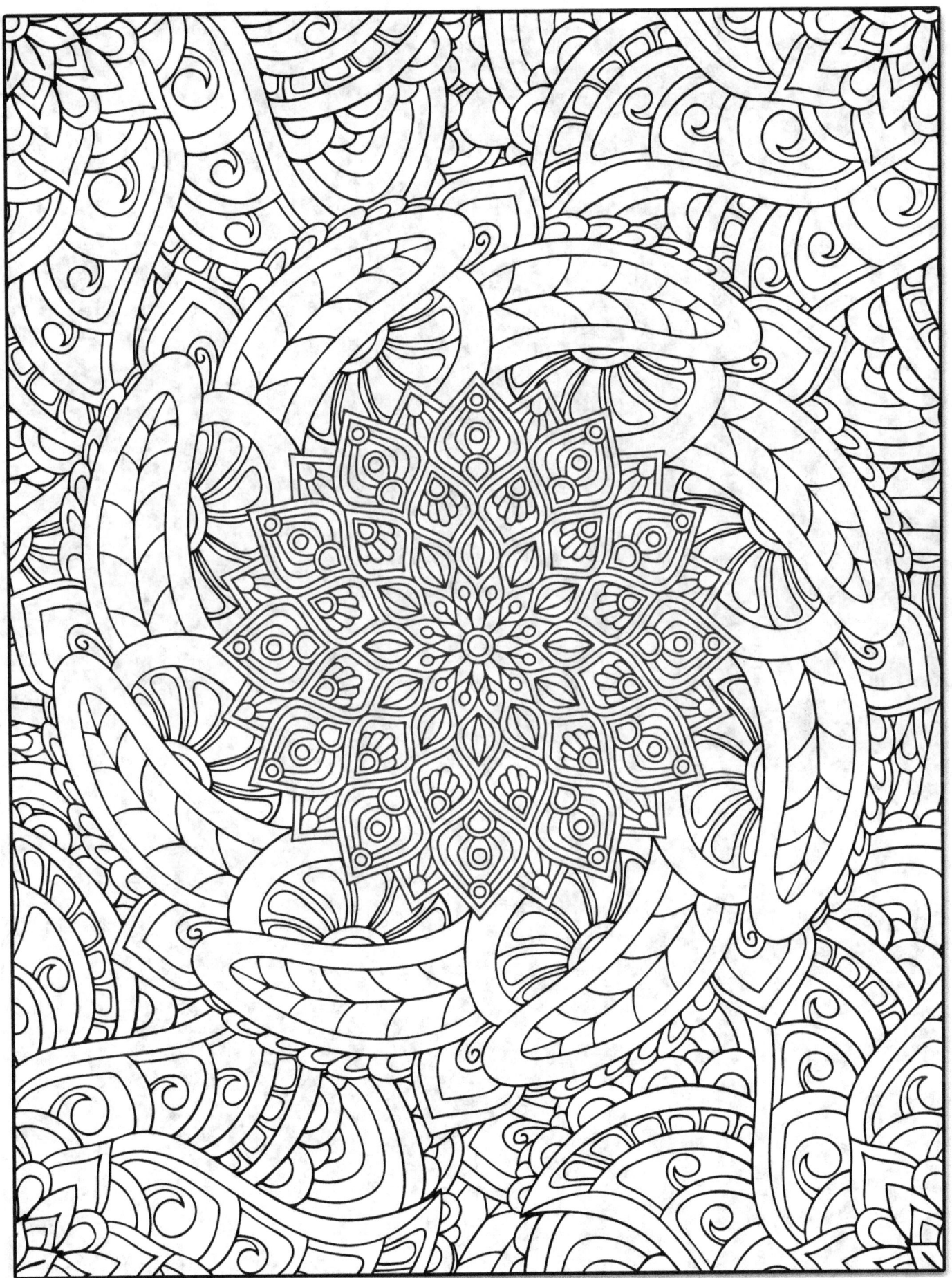

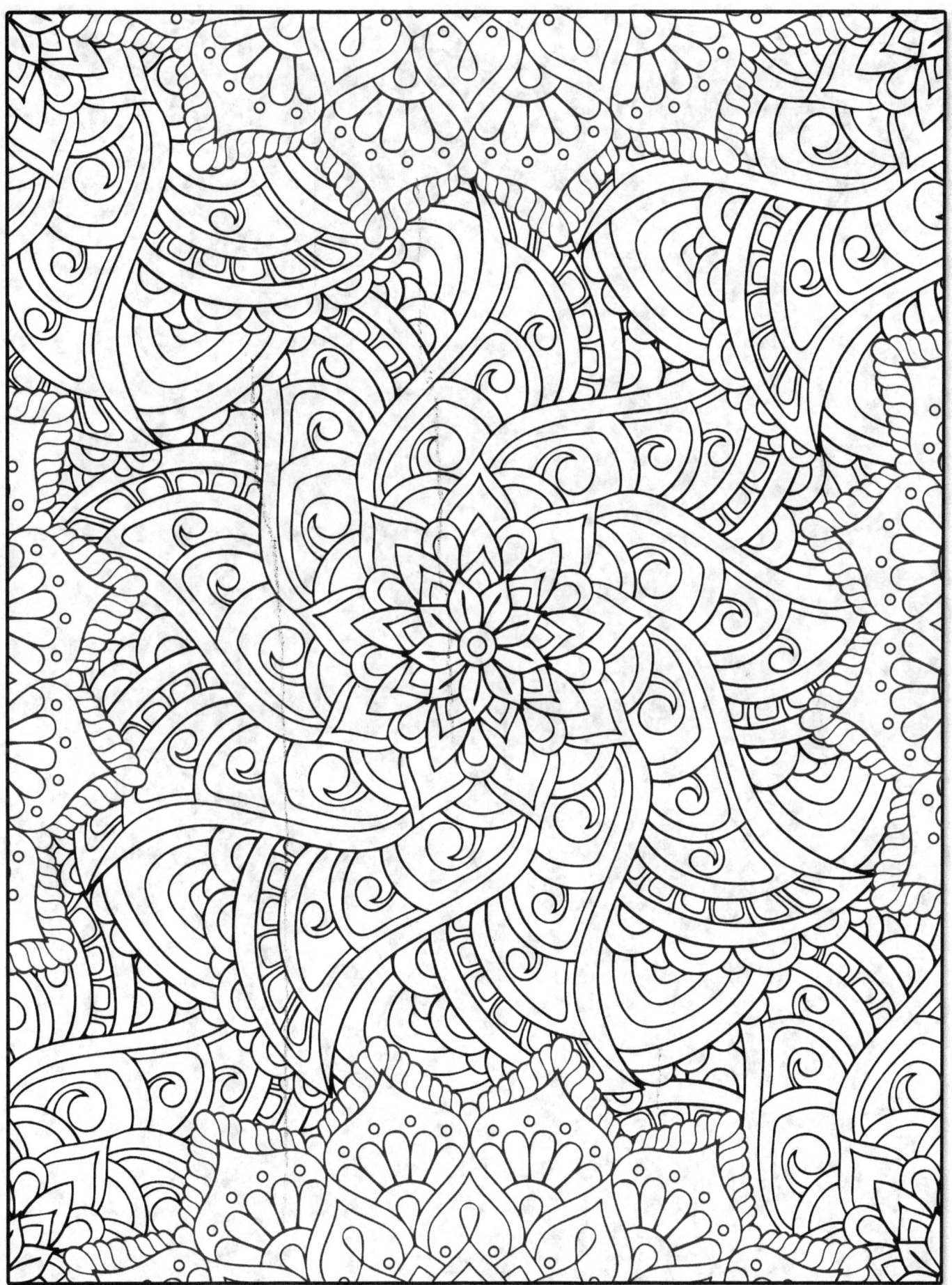

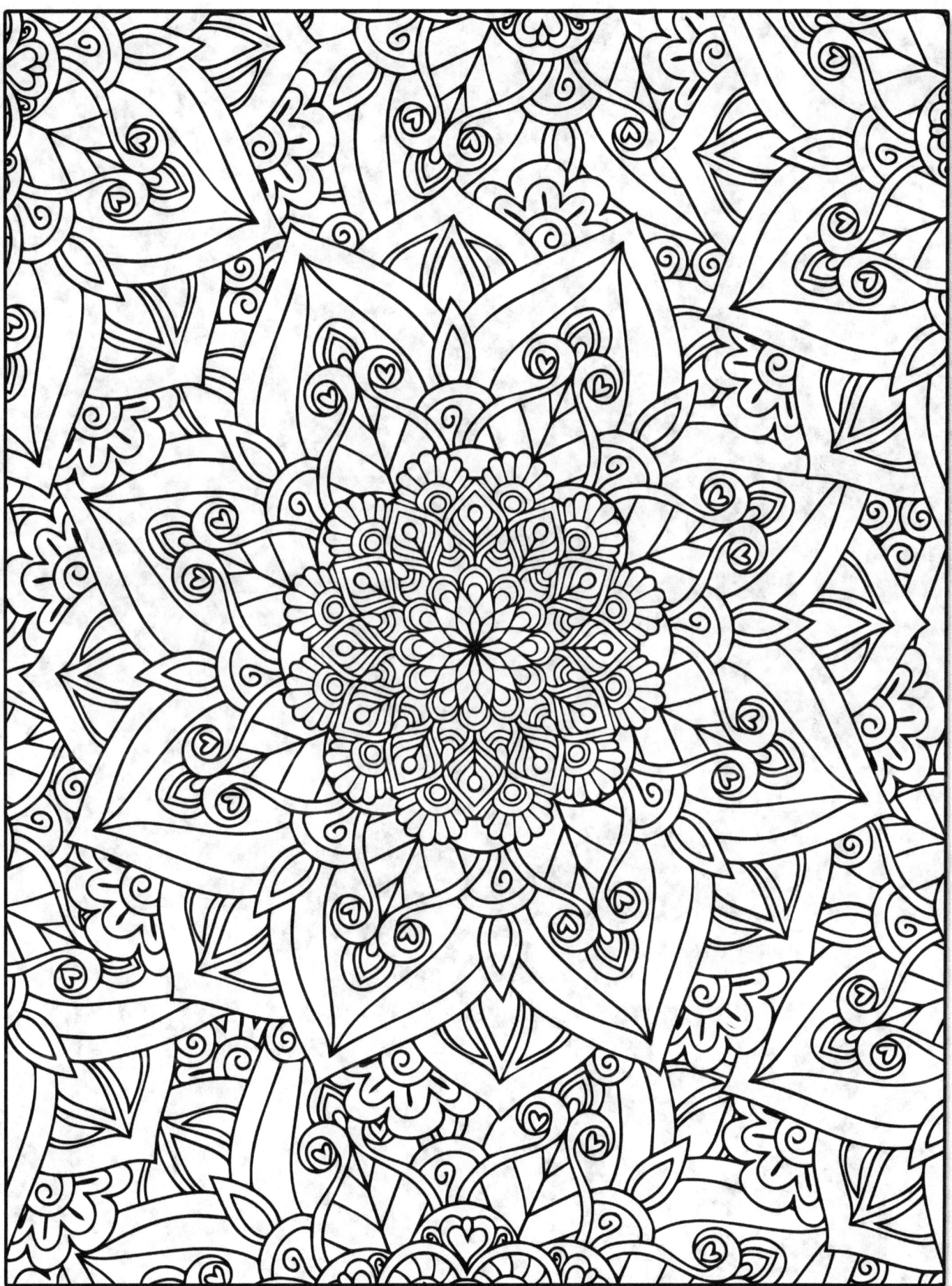

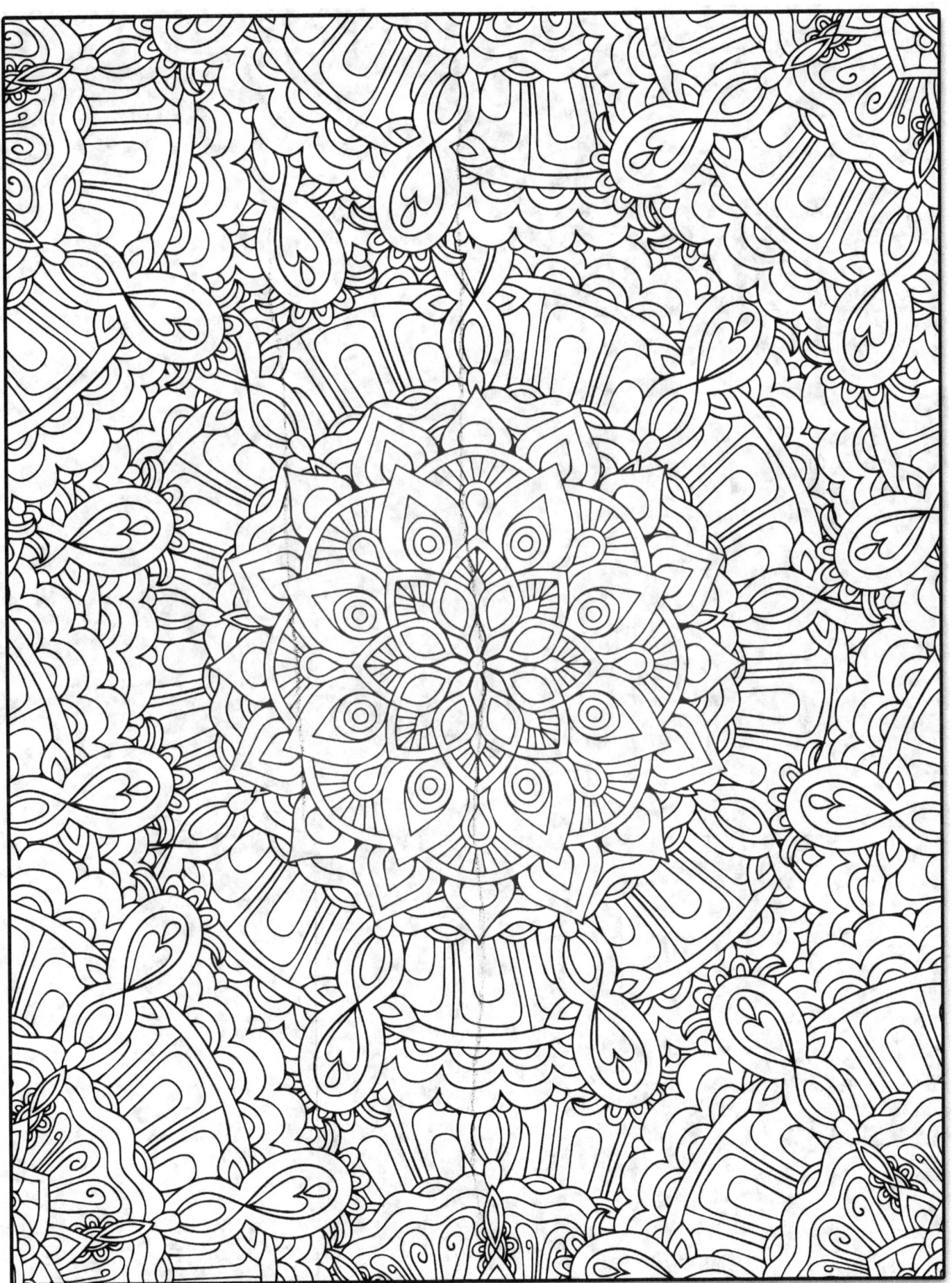

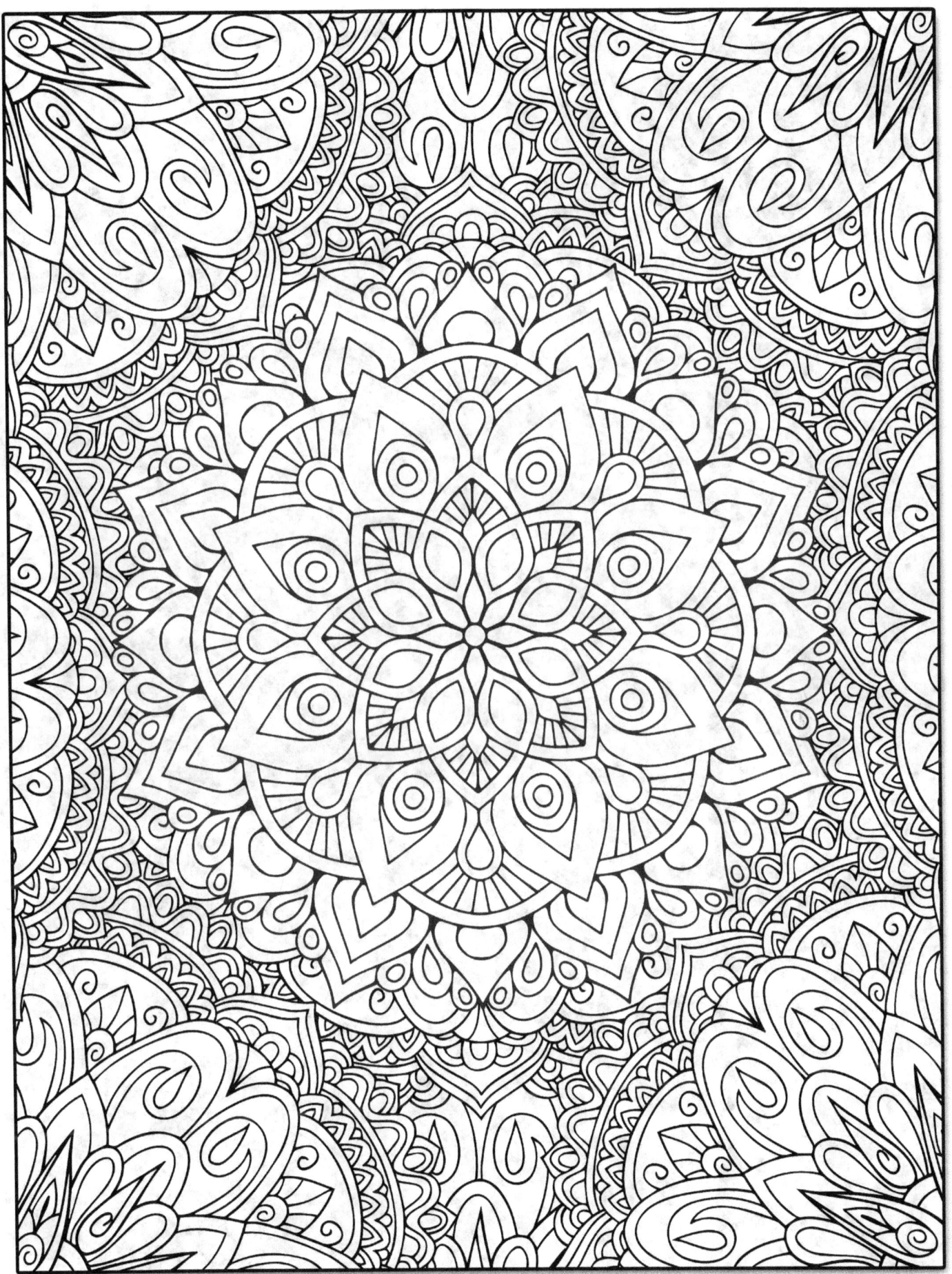

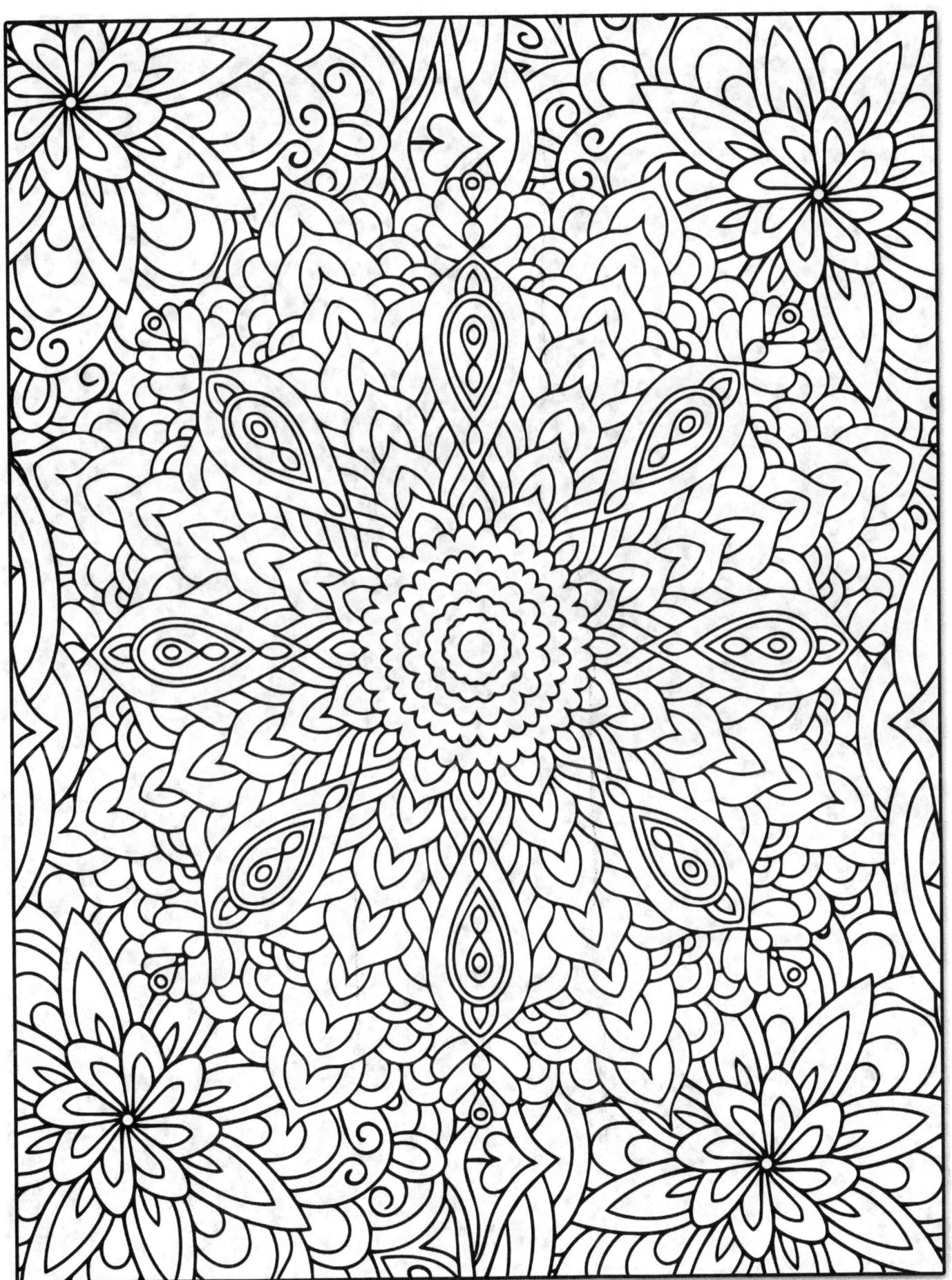

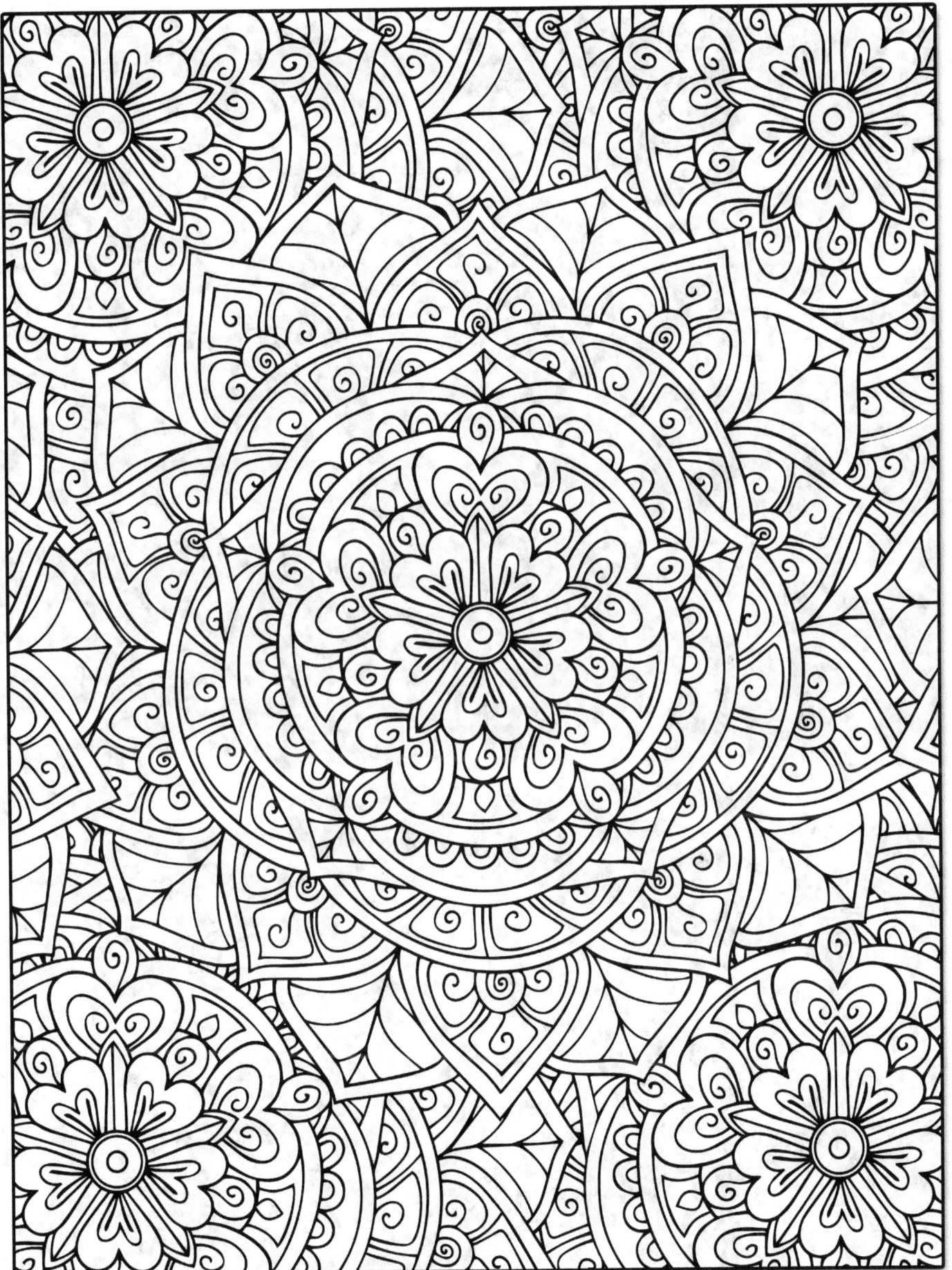

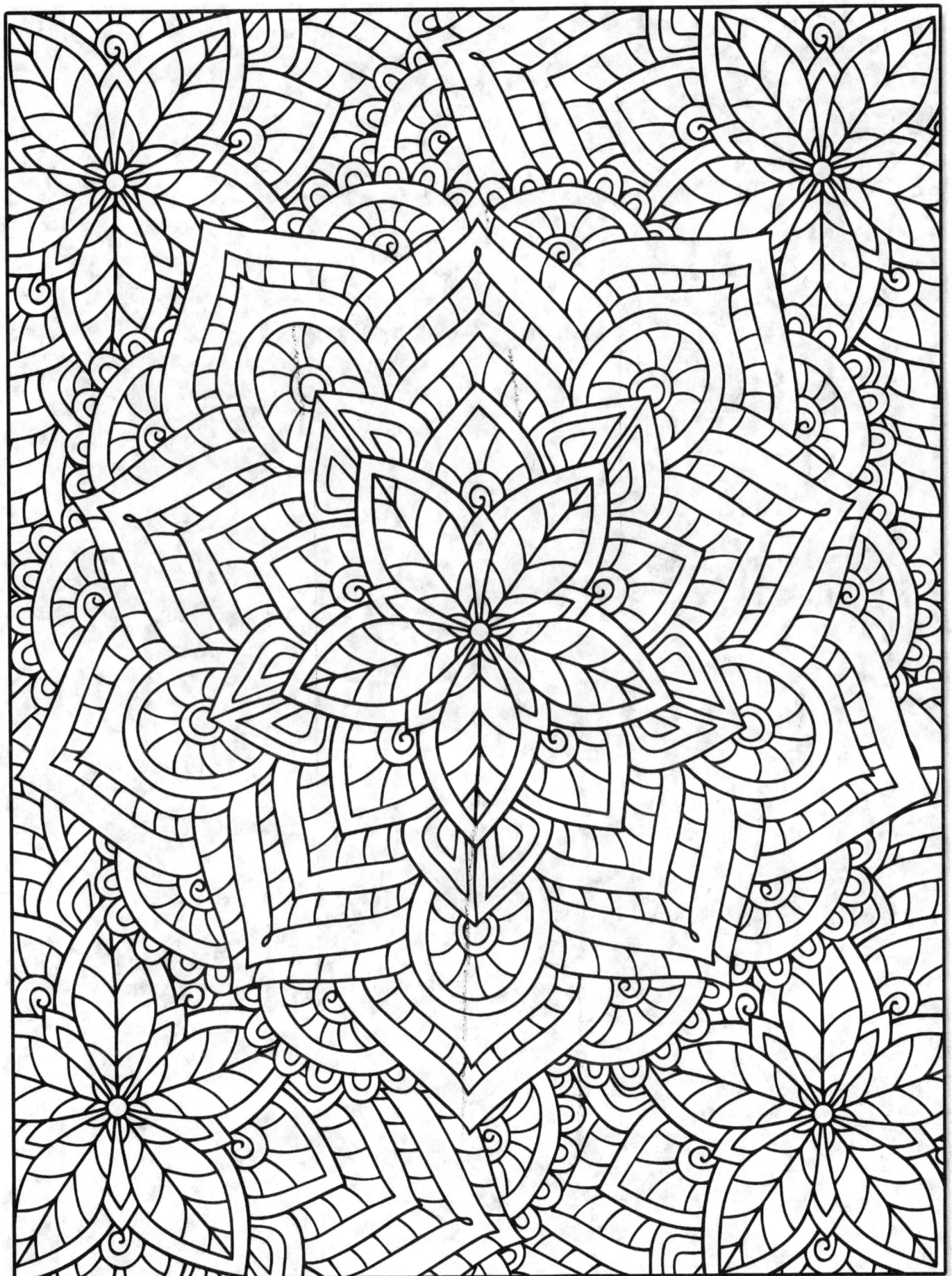

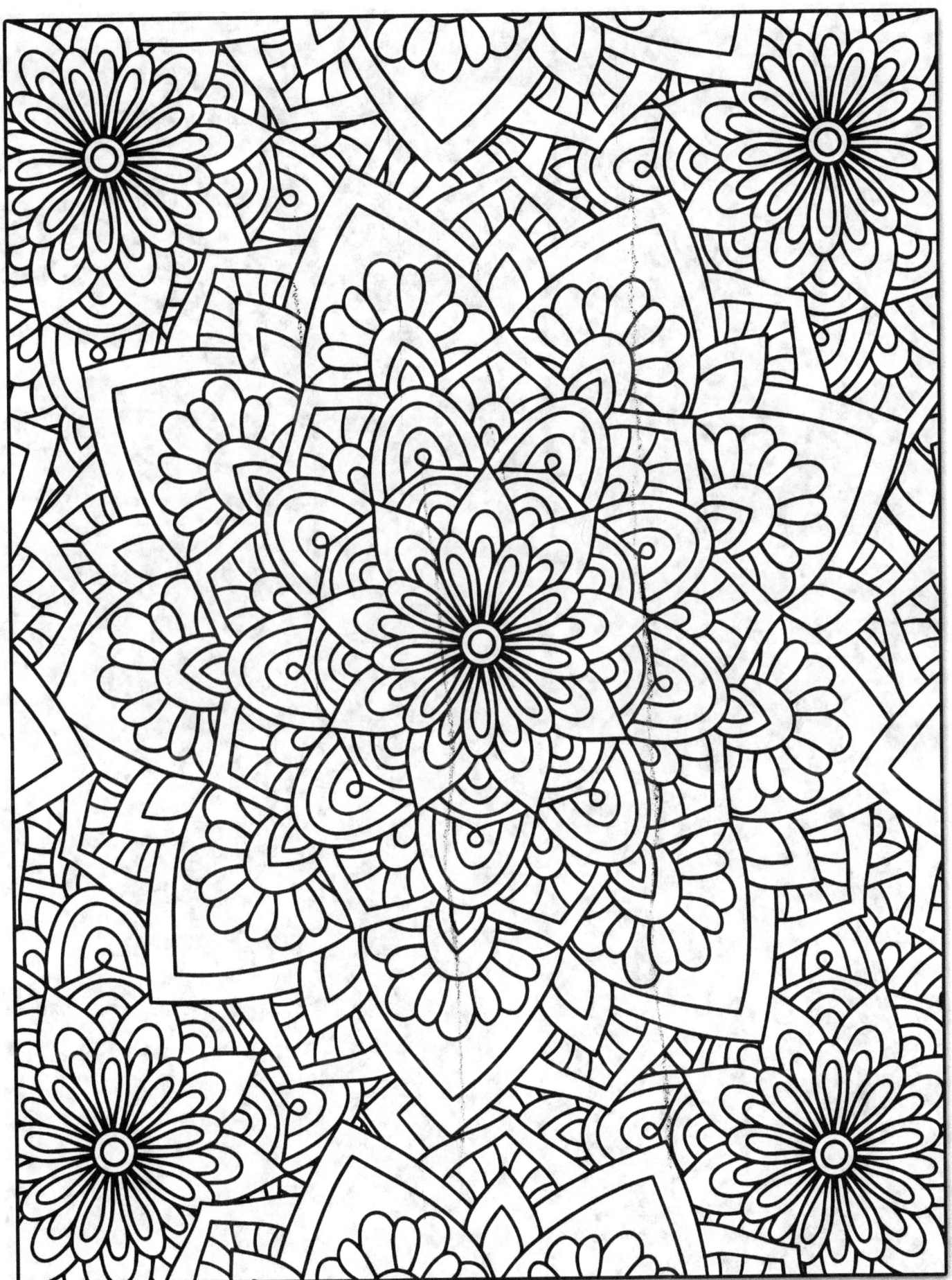

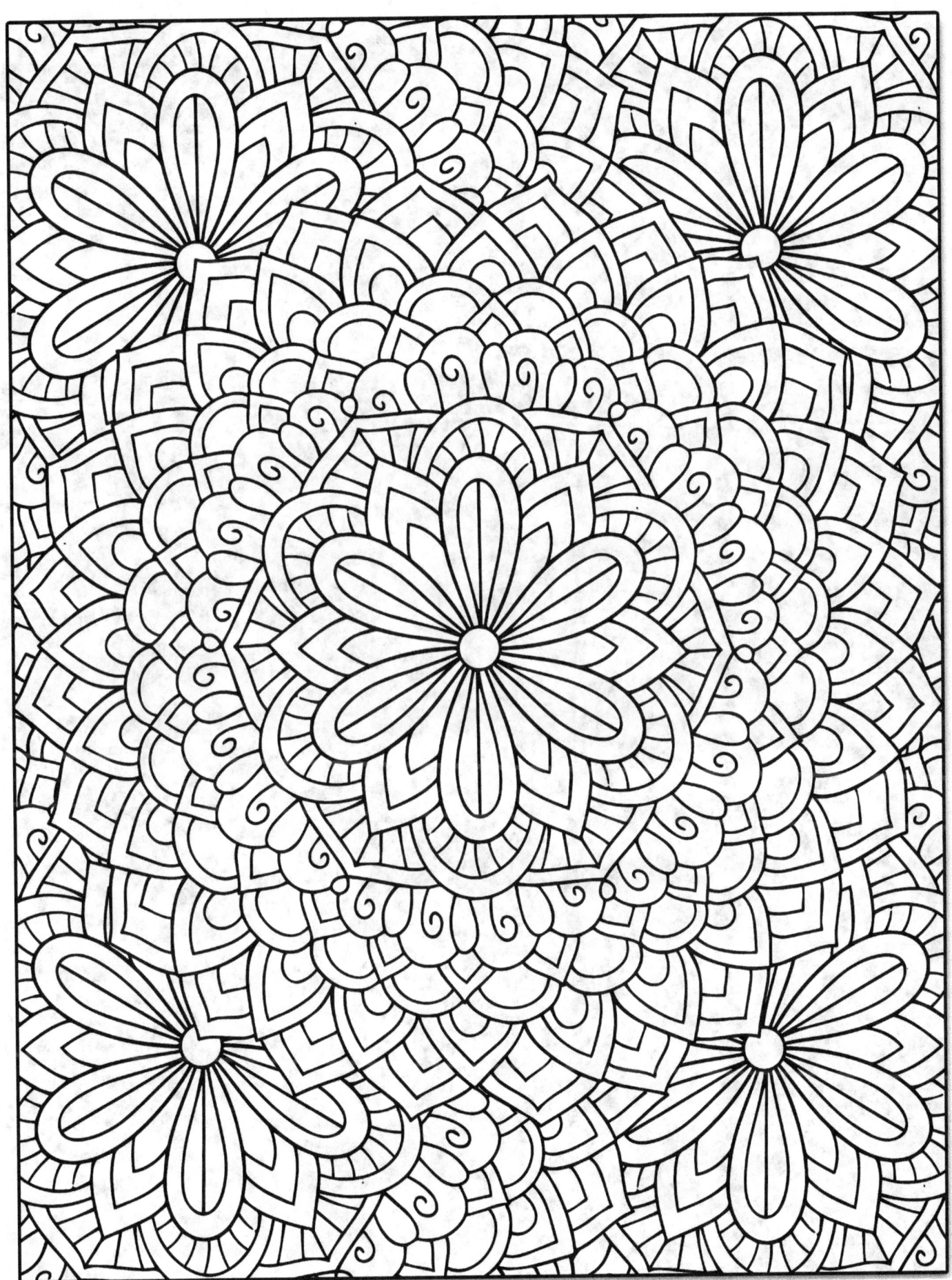

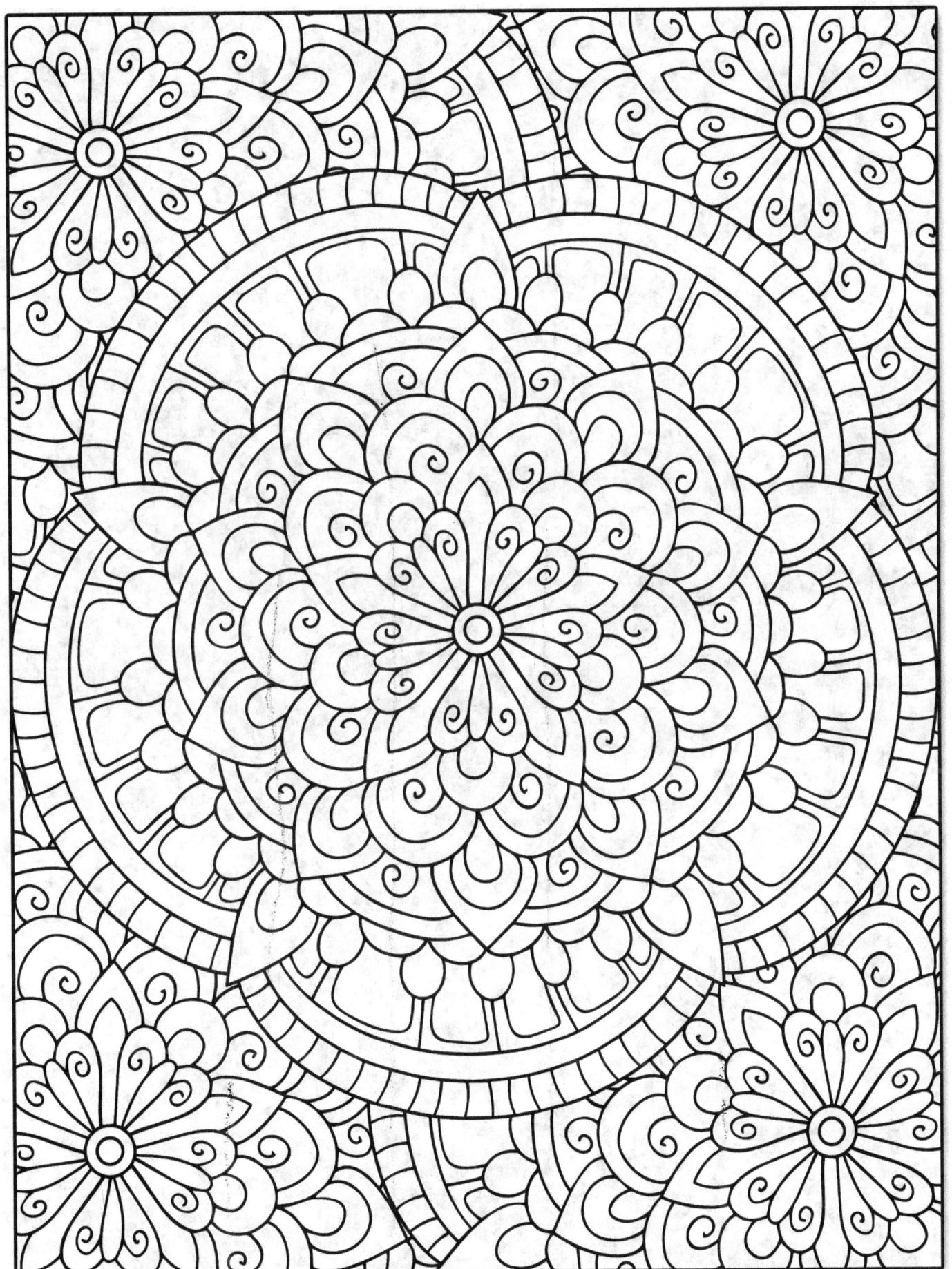

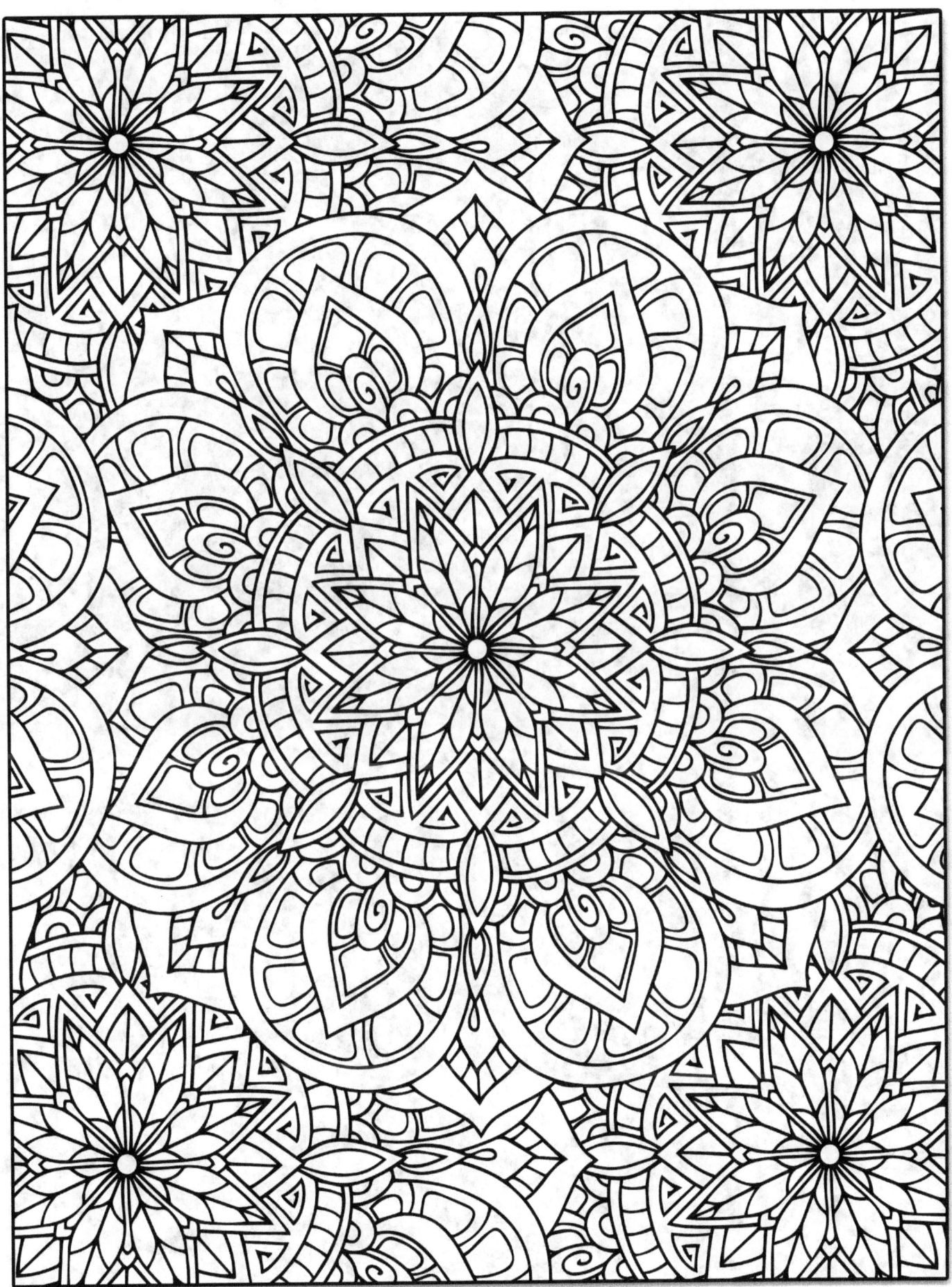

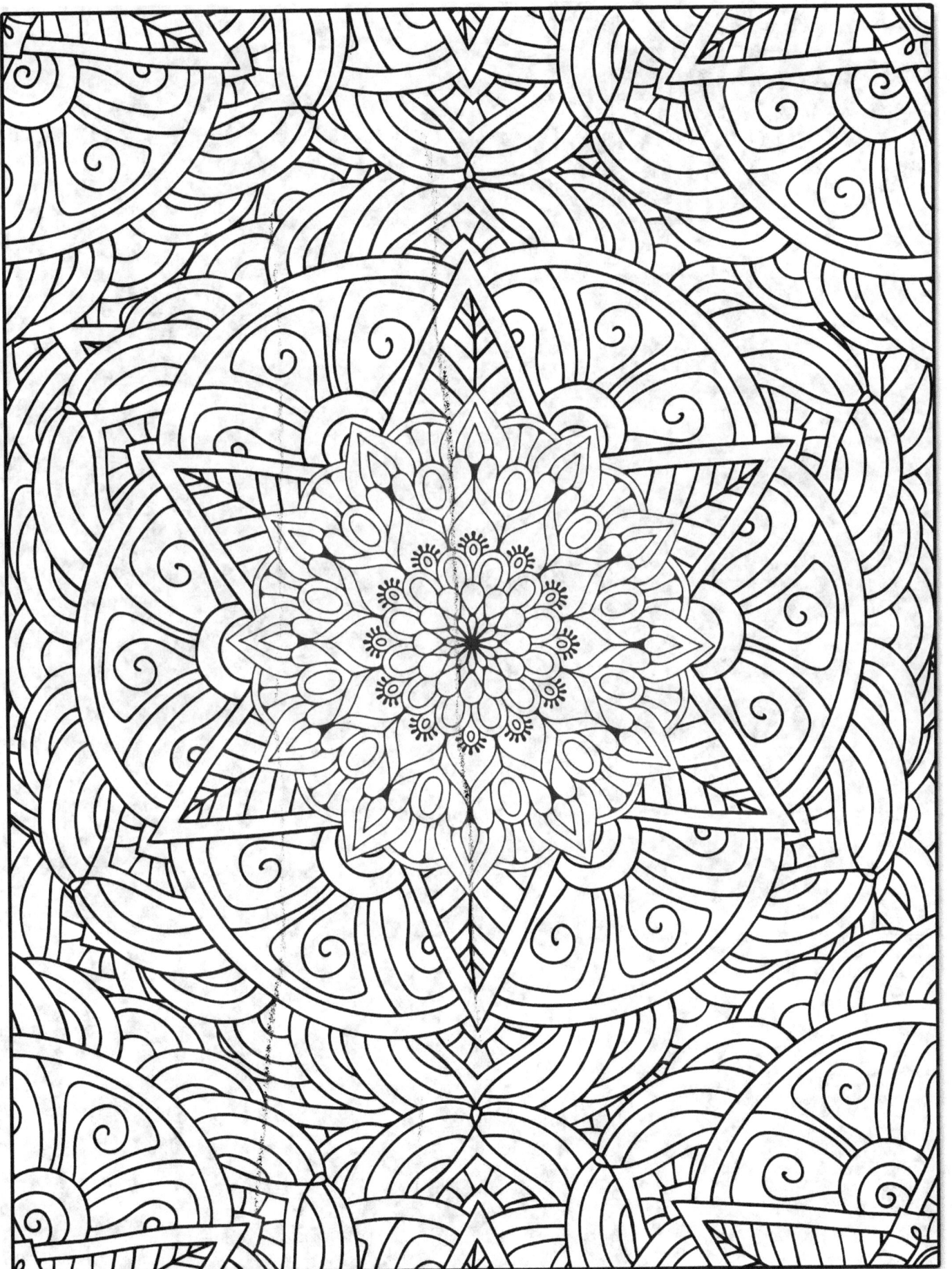

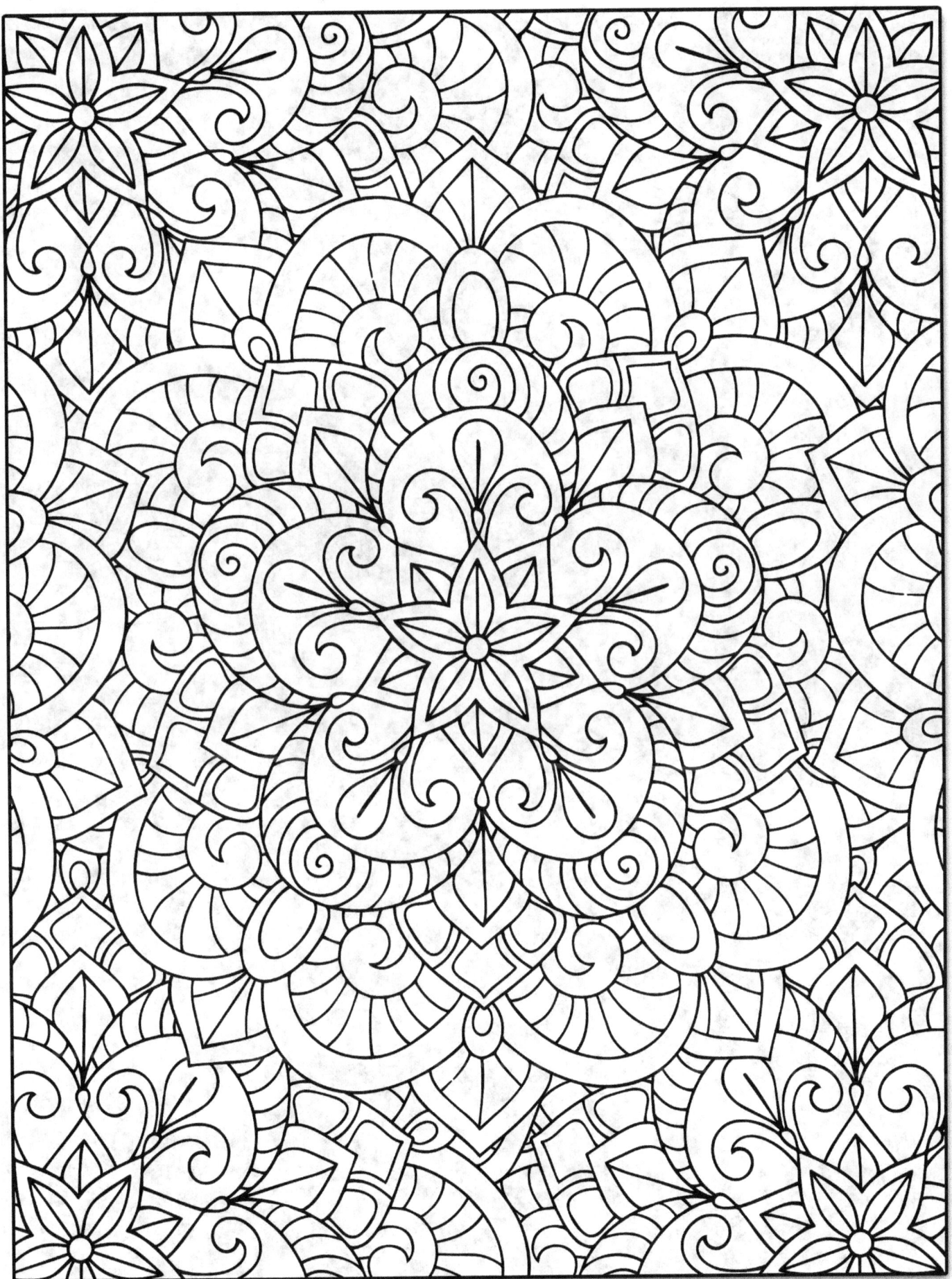

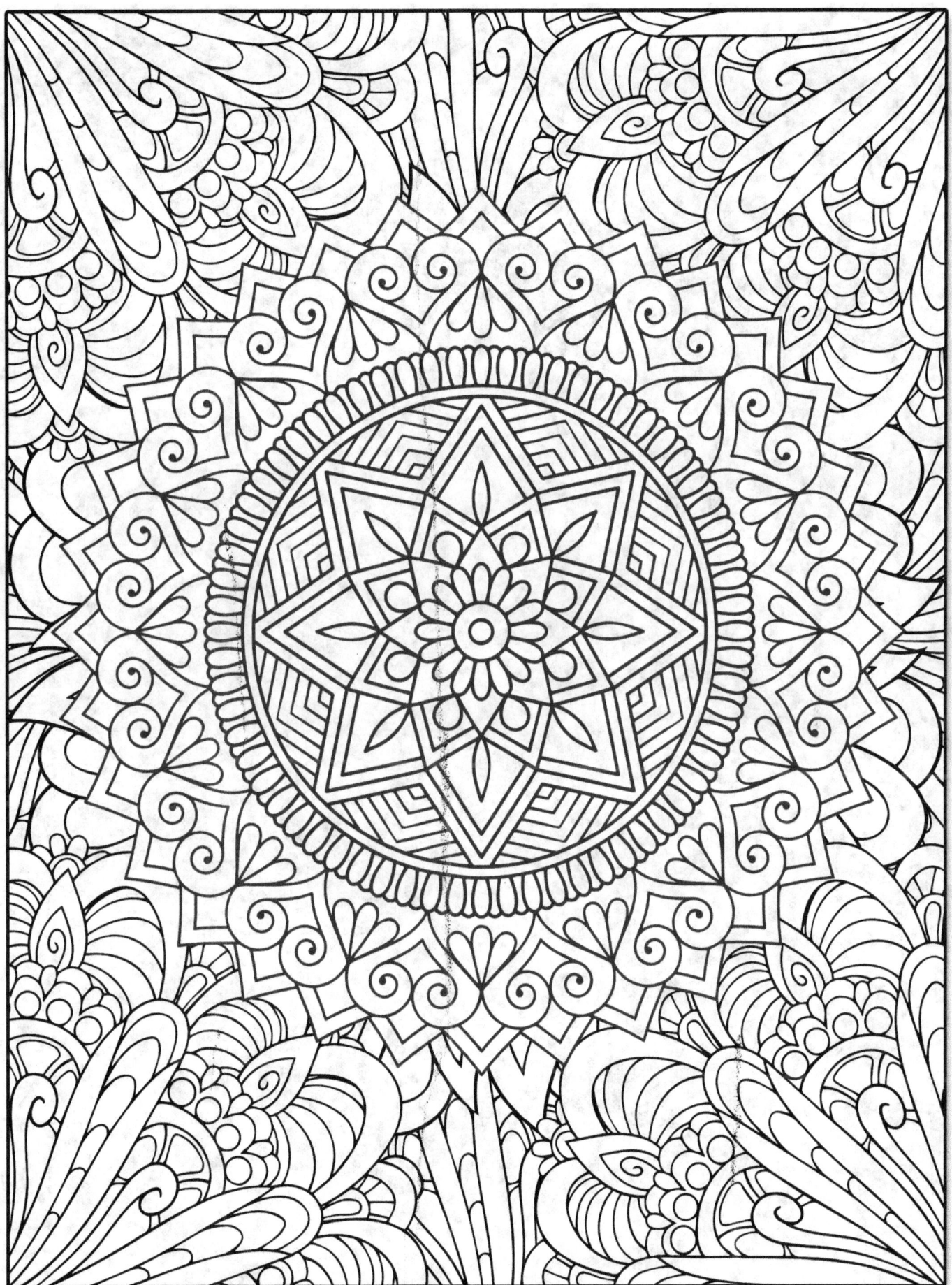

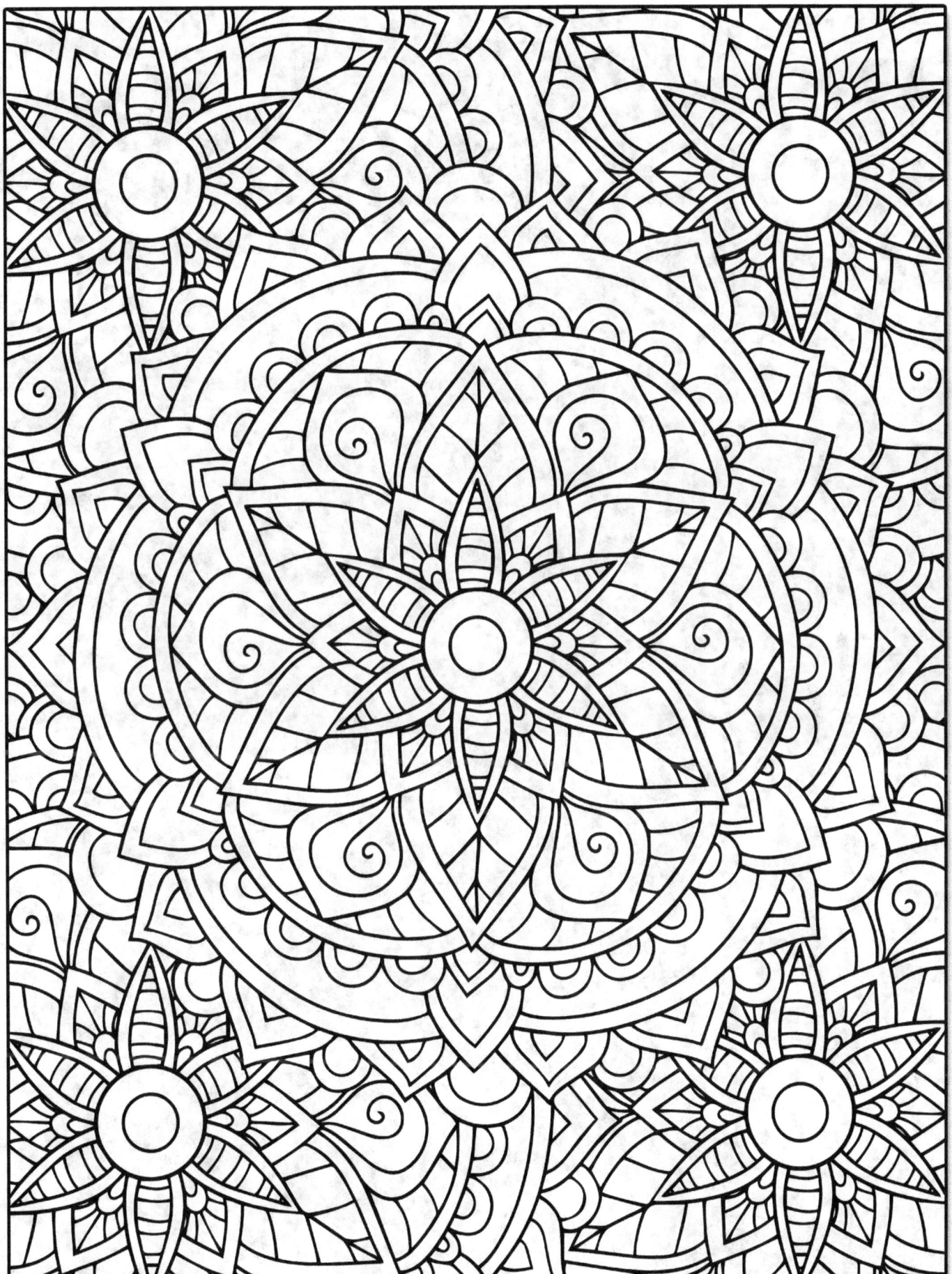

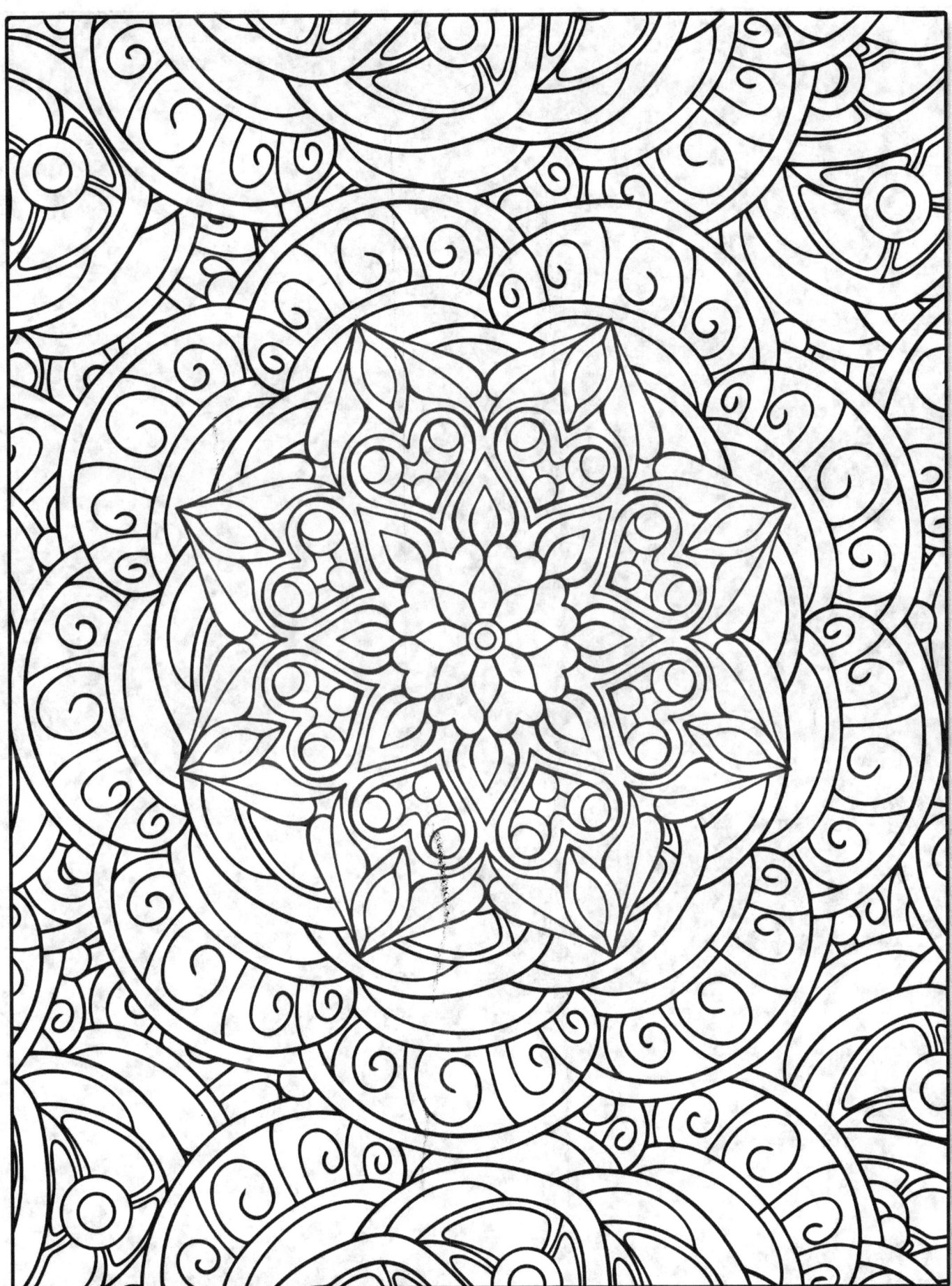

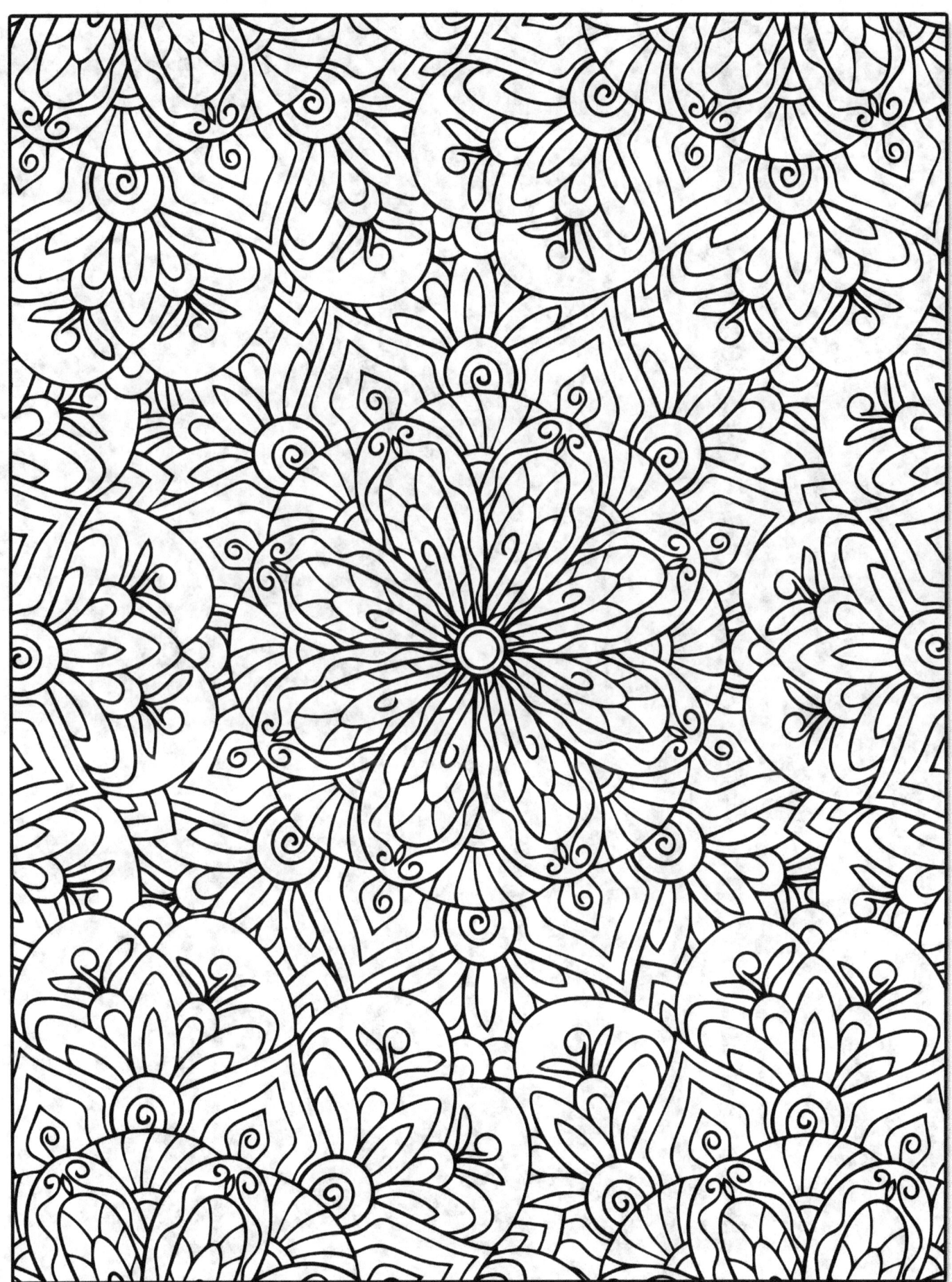

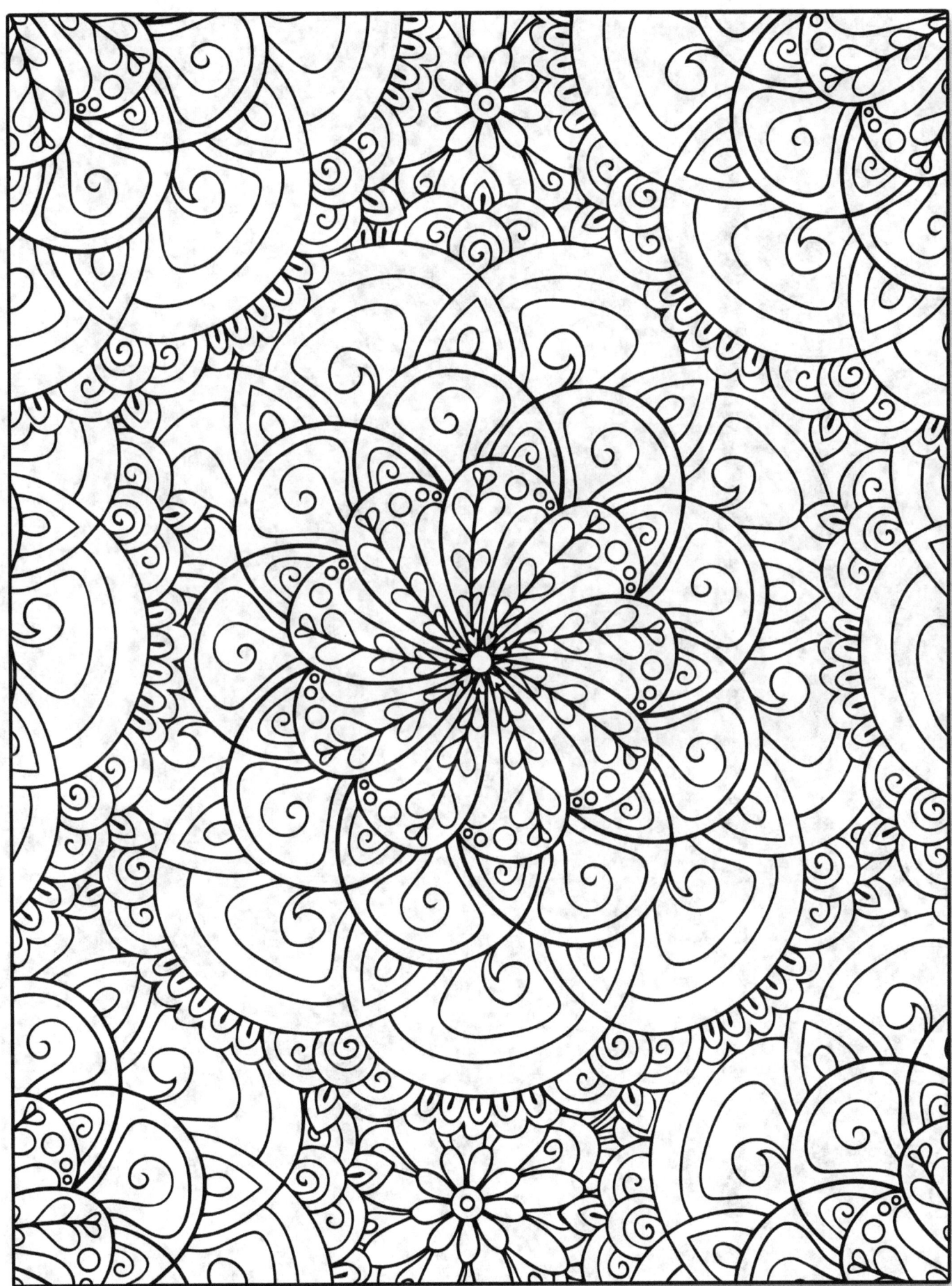

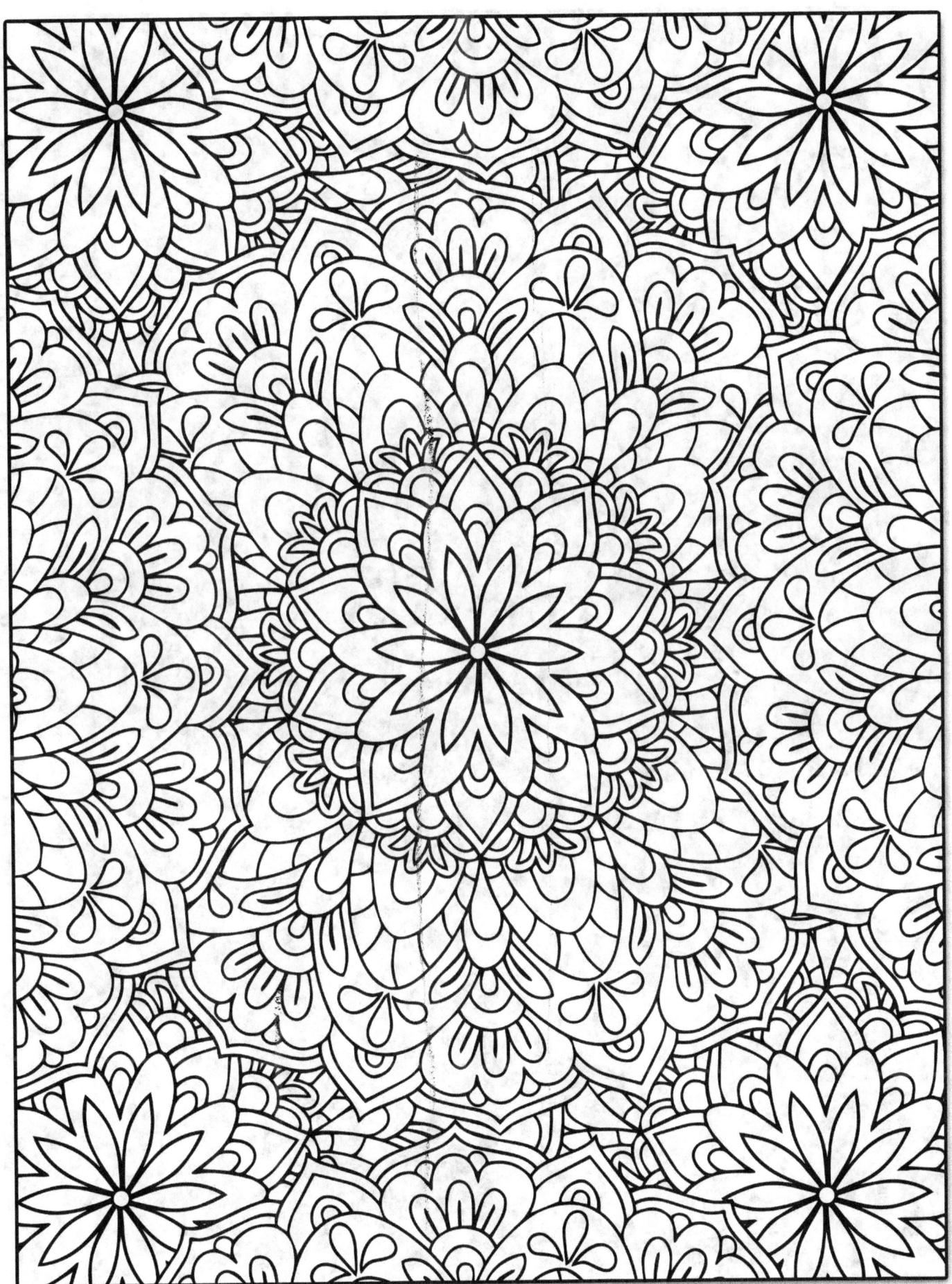

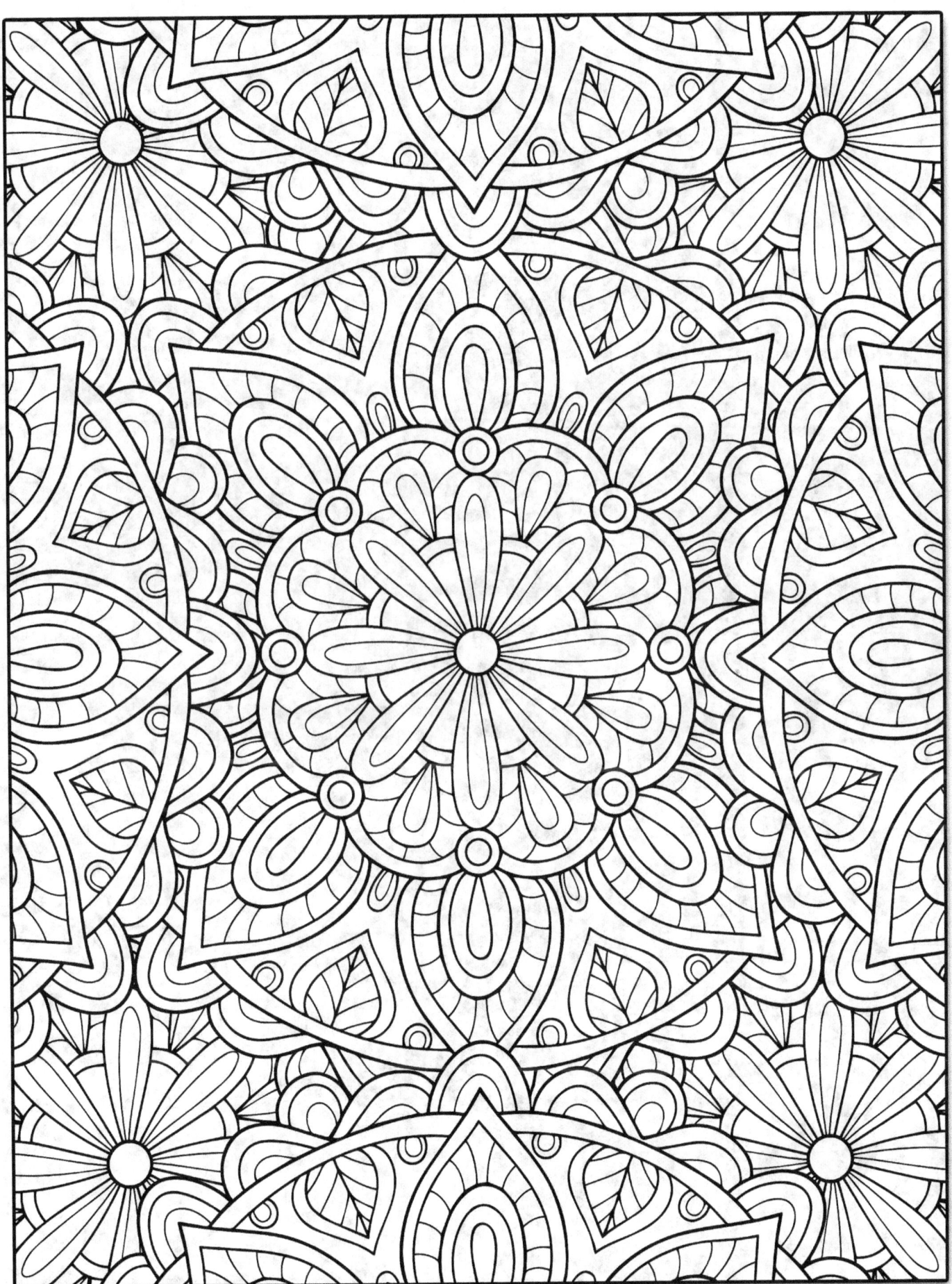

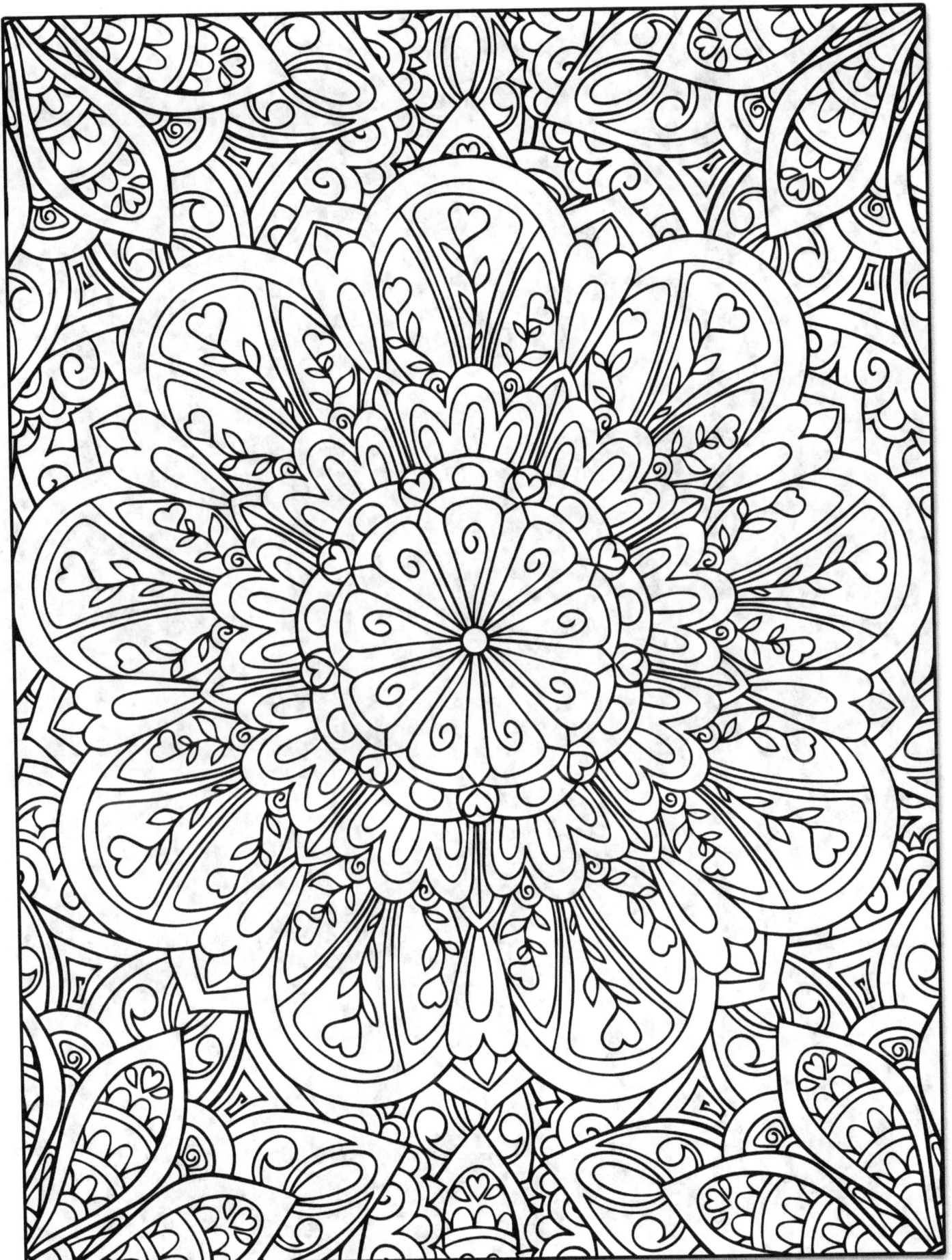

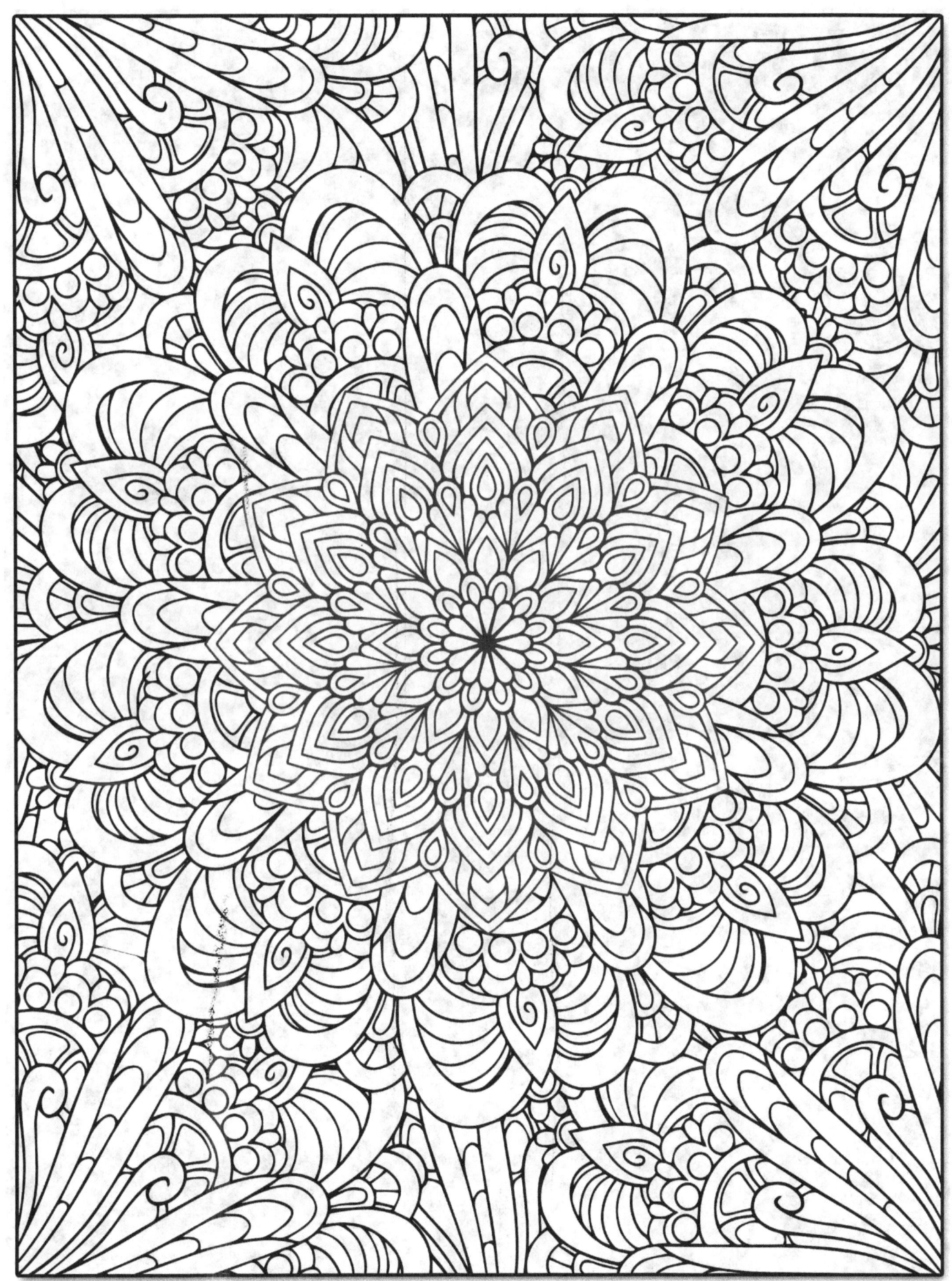

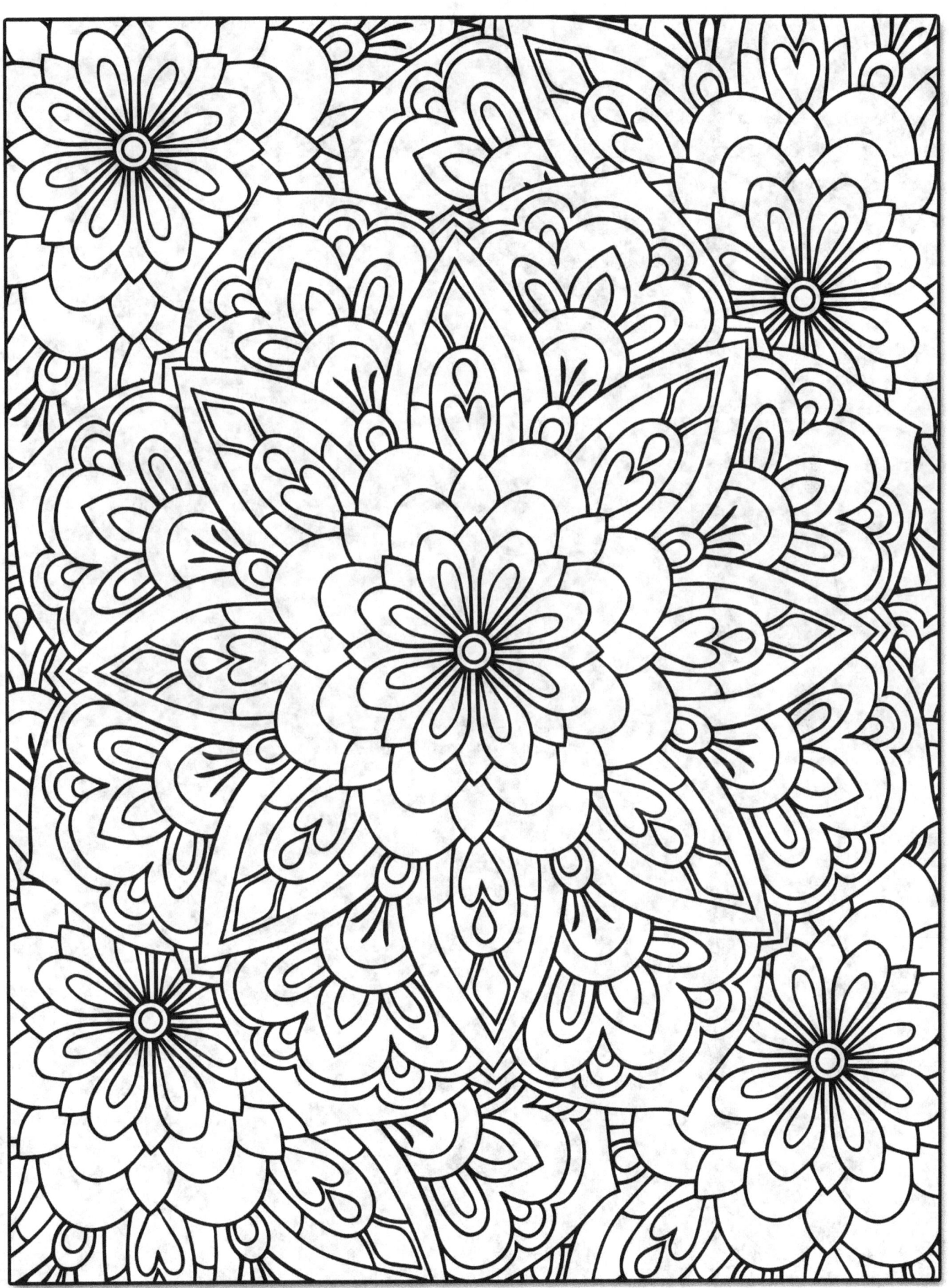

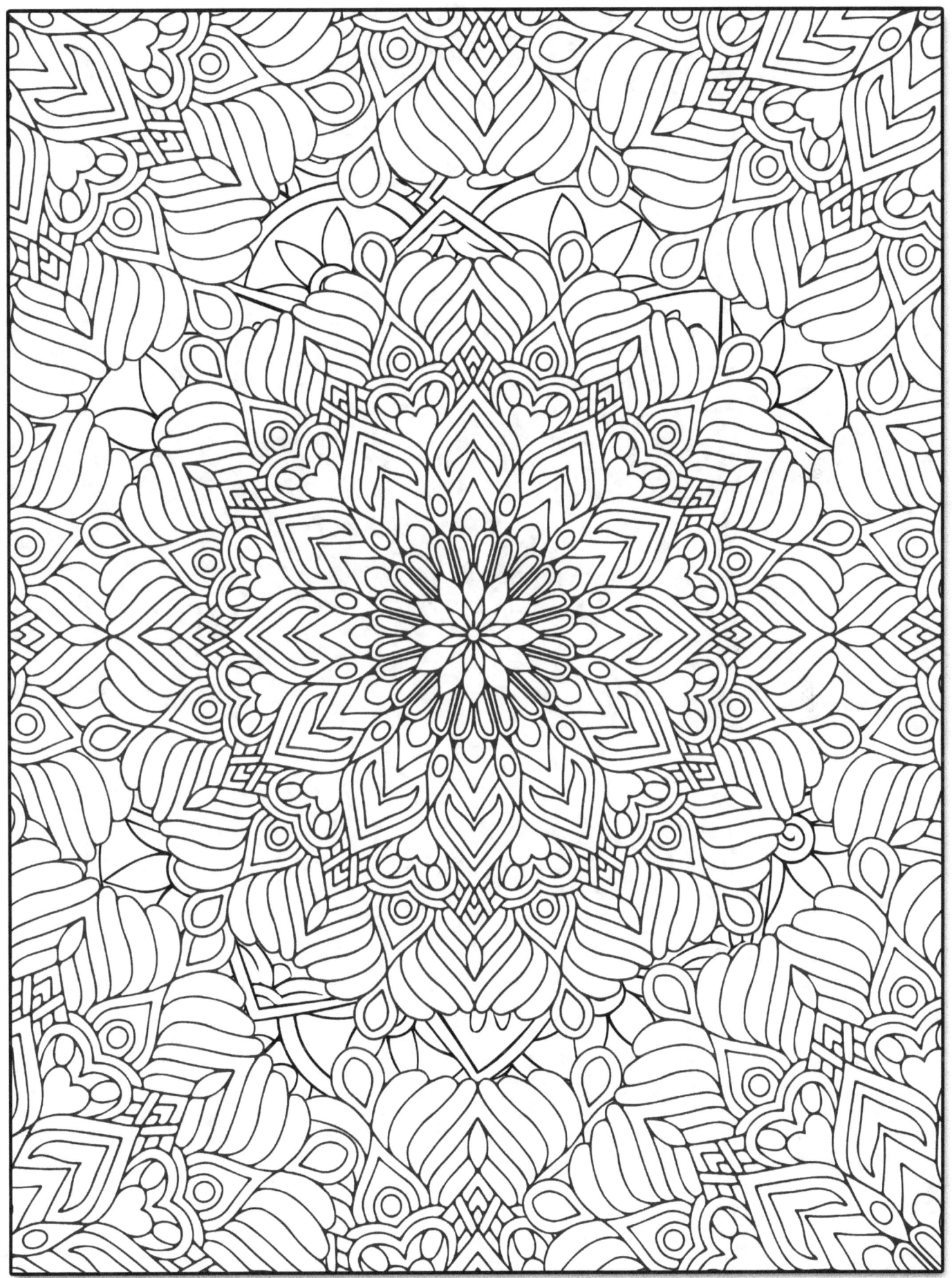